ABC

LITERACY STORYTIMES

Storytimes
to Promote
Literacy &
Learning

by Marilyn Lohnes

UpstartBooks

Fort Atkinson, Wisconsin

To little Sophie:
I hope we'll soon be able to practice these finger plays together.

And to Stephanie:
Thanks for lending a helping hand.

Published by UpstartBooks
W5527 State Road 106
P.O. Box 800
Fort Atkinson, Wisconsin 53538-0800
1-800-448-4887

© Marilyn Lohnes, 2008
Cover design and illustrations by Debra Neu

Although the bulk of the content of this book is original, every effort has been made to trace the ownership of any non-original copyrighted material. In the event of any question arising as to the use of any material, the editor and publisher, while expressing regret for any inadvertent error, will be happy to make the necessary corrections in future printings.

The paper used in this publication meets the minimum requirements of American National Standard for Information Sciences — Permanence of Paper for Printed Library Materials. ANSI/NISO Z39.48-1992.

Table of Contents

Introduction

Learning to read and write during the early school years is a thrilling experience for most children. But for those children who do not make good progress early on, learning can become a difficult and frustrating experience that can destroy self-confidence and even future success.

Teaching children to read and write is not a simple task. Although there are multiple theories about what is the best way to teach, most everyone can agree that early instruction with purposeful context allows children time to see and hear letters and words and to assemble the meaning of these collections. Children do not need to be a certain age in order to be exposed to letters and words. They begin learning language from the time they are born. Exposing children to a print-rich environment at an early age teaches them that there is a connection between spoken and written language, and that they can begin to learn them together rather than as two isolated events.

Early Literacy and Phonemic Awareness

The premise of all alphabetic languages is phonemic awareness—the understanding that speech consists of a sequence of sounds, known as phonemes. A phoneme determines the difference between words such as "big" and "dig." A child who is phonemically aware recognizes speech as a sequence of these small sounds, assembled together to create words and consequent comprehension. He or she can identify the individual sounds in the spoken word and can blend phonemes together to form words.

While units of sound are referred to as phonemes, the written versions are called graphemes. For example:

    l / i /p   contains 3 graphemes and 3 phonemes

    sh / i / p   contains 3 graphemes and 3 phonemes

    s / l / i / p contains 4 graphemes and 4 phonemes

When children are provided with explicit instruction in phonemic and graphemic awareness, they acquire skills in decoding sounds and letters and gain an early insight into the workings of our alphabetic writing system (Stanovich, 1986). Children who are aware of the sounds and written components of words are generally faster in mastering reading skills and are more confident in the entire learning process.

Creating a Stronger Literacy Link in Storytime

Typically storytime programs strengthen children's listening and speaking skills. They hear a story, identify patterns and repetition in rhymes and fingerplays, and use basic language forms to communicate their comprehension of the program. These are all crucial skills in preparing children to read and write, and are an excellent start in developing lifelong literacy habits.

Oh, but how much farther we can go! Most storytime programs neglect to consciously introduce letters and specific sounds into the formula. Before children can make sense of the alphabet, they need to understand that the sounds that are paired with the letters are one and the same as the sounds of speech. Children need to notice these sounds and to discover that a variety of these sounds exist. When sound and letter recognition are paired, the association between speaking, reading, and writing becomes much more evident. Children need to experiment with and manipulate letters to make words and create meaning. Early spelling exposure is a powerful means of leading children to internalize phonemic awareness and the alphabetic principle. The predictability of a storytime program guides children to connect and expect letter and word association with spoken words and objects.

There are three steps to include in a storytime program to create a stronger literacy link:

1. **Hearing the Sounds**

   Children are encouraged to listen carefully for the first letter sound in a word. They can practice the sound the letter makes, and can think of more words that have a similar sound at the beginning.

   The next step is to teach the separate phonemes in a word (i.e.: b, i, r, d). One should not expect a preschooler to correctly spell an introduced word, but to simply be aware of the different letters and sounds held within.

When blended together the individual sounds or letters create words.

2. **Reading the Letter**

   After identifying the sound of a letter, children can be taught to recognize the printed version of the letter and its sound.

3. **Writing the Letter**

   After hearing and reading the letters, children need to be given the opportunity to write individual letters. Since motor skills are still developing in the preschool years, one should not expect a masterful "w" or a perfect "g," but children should be introduced to the specific shapes the letters make to help with future identification. Later steps will include writing words and reading words.

The Finger Play in a Literacy Program

Finger plays introduce young children to poetry and the important elements of rhyme, sequence, and predictability. Together with book reading and other components of a storytime program, they create a learning atmosphere vital during the impressionable years of the young, pre-reading child. Although we don't necessarily think of finger plays as a literacy preparation, they are exactly that.

Finger play characters, or finger puppets, are visual elements that help children to associate spoken words with objects. As the adult chants "this little piggy," the child is delighted to actually see five little pig finger play characters perched atop a glove. As the word "pig" is repeated through the storytime, the association becomes even more clear.

Taking It Farther—Spelling with the Finger Play Glove

Inarguably, one of the best foundations for success in early reading is the familiarity of the letters of the alphabet. Children can sing the alphabet song, chant the letters, and point to the individual letters in a printed version of the alphabet. But do they fully understand each letter, or have they simply memorized the order? If you were to mix the letters of the alphabet up and place them in a row, would the child recognize each letter, or would they chant the rehearsed "ABCs" regardless of the arrangement? Children need to recognize the individual letters as unique elements that can be arranged in any order. By introducing simple graphemes to children, they become aware of the unlimited use of letters and the importance of them in reading and writing.

In a storytime setting the finger play glove can be used to introduce small words. With a pictorial representation of the word in the center of the glove, the word can be spelled above the picture. As letters are added, the picture of the object becomes less significant, and the letters become the elements to focus on. With the routine of a storytime program, children will quickly become aware of the significance of the letters in relation to early reading.

Basic Presentation Tips for Finger Plays

You can effectively present a new finger play by following these simple guidelines:

1. Select a finger play that you are comfortable with yourself. It is not advisable to pick one which you dislike or find awkward simply because it fits your theme. Children are quite quick to pick up on your enthusiasm, or lack thereof. Ensure that the rhyme flows well and does not contain words or phrases difficult for children to grasp. Feel free to alter any rhyme you see to have it better suit your own rhythm and style.

2. Rehearse the rhyme well. The rhyme tends to flow much better if you know beforehand precisely where to intonate or emphasize.

3. Using the characters, demonstrate the finger play yourself. Go through the entire rhyme, pausing only momentarily where predictable responses might be given by the children. Be sure to clearly enunciate the words.

4. Invite children to participate with hands and voices as you repeat the rhyme. You can either relay one line at a time, having the children repeat your words, or you can very slowly present the entire rhyme, allowing time for the children to join in the predictable and familiar phrases.

5. Once you have slowly gone through the rhyme with the children, you can repeat it at a more normal pace, thus encouraging full participation from the children.

A Literacy Storytime Template

Children enjoy variety in their stories and rhymes, but they generally respond best to a routine in the storytime presentation. In this way, they are prepared for the next activity and consequently feel more involved and willing to participate in the overall program. The following is a suggested routine, designed for preschool to grade one and would run approximately 30 minutes without the alphabet and creative activities, and 45–60 minutes with these components added.

30-Minute Program

1. **Opening**

   This may be achieved with an opening song that is repeated at the beginning of each storytime. You can also introduce storytime with a puppet, or with any other activity that signifies to the children the start of a program. It prepares them for the upcoming stories and activities that require their attention.

2. **Introductory Poem (introduction of theme)**

   A brief poem introduces the theme, and the sounds of that word, emphasizing the beginning letter: *He starts with "s" and ends with "nake," and "sss, sss, sss" is the sound he'll make.*

3. **Finger Play Spelling**

   The theme word is then spelled out for the children. This can be done on a blackboard, or a flannelboard, but I prefer to use the finger play glove (see instructions on page 13). Beginning with the first letter of the word, slowly add letters, pausing between each one to focus on the sounds and the blends: *s, sn, sna, snak, snake.* Once the word has been spelled, the word can be emphasized.

4. **Name Game (alliteration)**

   To develop phonemic awareness children are encouraged to think of other words that start with the same sound as the featured word or topic. For example, if "snake" is the featured theme, children could suggest "spider, sheep, squirrel," etc. With the help of the facilitator, children can create silly sentences, incorporating the names of children in the program (i.e.: Sammy the snake screams when he sees spiders.). The sillier the sentences are, the more fun the children will have.

5. **First Story**

   The first story should be the longest one, as children have just assembled and have their longest attention span at this point. Read clearly, making sure to enunciate words fully. Ask questions about the story to determine comprehension.

6. **First Finger Play**

   Select a rhyme suitable to your theme that you would enjoy presenting as much as the children would enjoy hearing. Select a rhyme that encourages participation through chanting of repeated words or predictable responses. Repeat the rhyme, encouraging the children to participate.

7. **Second Story**

   The second story should be the most varied story, either in its content or in its presentation. A flannelboard, cut-and-tell, or draw-and-tell story works well here, as does the telling of a story with puppets or other props. Encourage participation with words or actions. For example, if the story involves pulling, as in the case of *The Enormous Turnip*, have the children pretend to pull as they chant, "they pulled, and they pulled, and they pulled."

8. **Active Rhyme/Stretch**

   Most likely at this point in the program little bottoms will be shifting and toes will be wiggling. Invite the children to stand up and participate in an active rhyme or song. A number of suitable songs exist, or you might try this simple, adapted traditional rhyme:

   I wiggle my fingers,

   I wiggle my toes.

   I wiggle my bottom,

   I wiggle my nose.

   I think that the wiggles,

   Are all out of me.

   So now I can sit

   And hear a story.

9. **Second Finger Play**

   Select a gentle rhyme with soft, predictable responses.

10. **Third Story**

    The final story to the program should be short and simple, and should focus on simple text or rhyme schemes. Children are beginning to tire at this point and do not concentrate well on longer stories with more complicated plots. It should be a fun and entertaining story.

    Closing if not using alphabet and creative activities

    Have some specific way of indicating to the children that the storytime is over.

A closing song such as "Storytime Is Over Now" is a suitable finale, as is a simple announcement. You may choose to give each child a special hand stamp to signify the closing.

The **Alphabet Activities,** along with the **Practice Printing sheet**, can be provided as handouts for children and parents to work on together at home.

45- to 60-Minute Program

In addition to steps 1–10, add the following:

11. Alphabet Activities

Connect-the-dot patterns using alphabet letters continue to promote the awareness of the letters of the alphabet. Though the pattern of reading is left to right, the alphabet letters may be in different places. This encourages the children to recognize the letters alone, and not as a pattern. Give each child a connect-the-dot pattern based on the theme, and encourage each child to go through the letters of the alphabet to create the picture.

Additional activities incorporating matching of letters or placing of letters further strengthens the alphabet awareness. Children may work individually on these pictures, or the pictures may be enlarged to create a classroom activity.

12. Creative Activities

Simple craft and activities related to the theme encourage participation and are fun for the children to do. Finishing the program with a memorable craft will remind children of the pleasures of these programs, and will encourage them to want to participate again.

13. Closing

As with the 30-minute program, have some specific way of indicating to the children that the storytime is over.

The **Practice Printing sheet** can be provided as a handout for children and parents to work on together at home. Remember: it's just for fun! A perfect mastery of printing at this age is neither expected nor encouraged.

Using the Glove and Characters

The glove is as essential to finger play and spelling presentation as the characters themselves. It creates a visual background from which the characters or letters appear or disappear. It also becomes a focal point for children as they become familiar with program routines. When you place the glove on your hand, children become instantly aware that a word is going to be spelled, or a finger play rhyme will soon follow, and will pay careful attention to discover which characters or letters will appear.

Most presenters wear the glove on the hand that is not their writing hand. This allows him or her to manipulate the letters and characters more comfortably with the dominant hand. Once the glove is in place, the characters are introduced.

Word Spelling

For word spelling, a character is placed in the center velcro tab of the glove. One-by-one, the letters of the word are added from left to right on the glove. The presenter pauses between each letter, focusing on the sounds and the blends. Once the word has been achieved, the word is spelled by pointing to the letters and saying them out loud.

Finger Play Rhymes

For rhymes, finger play characters are introduced in one of the following three ways:

1. **Count Down Rhyme**

   If the finger rhyme begins with five characters, working down to none, place all five characters on the velcro tabs of the glove. Encourage the children to count as you add the characters. Begin your rhyme and remove a character at the appropriate spot in the finger play. Simply pull the character free from the glove and "hide" it by wrapping your fingers around it. It will appear to the children that you are making a fist. After you begin the next verse, casually place the removed character on your lap and prepare for removing the next one. When your rhyme is finished, you may take advantage of the counting component again by asking the children to count with you as you put the characters away.

2. **Count Up Rhyme**

   If the finger rhyme begins with one character and works up to five, start by placing the characters in your lap. Hold up one character and introduce the rhyme before attaching it to the glove. As the rhyme calls for another character, pick up one from your lap and attach it to your glove. Again, when the rhyme is finished, you may ask the children to help you count the characters as they are put away.

3. **Stay and Play Rhyme**

Occasionally rhymes call for five characters initially with none being removed (i.e.: "This Little Piggy"). In this case, place all five characters on the velcro tabs of the glove as with the count down rhyme. Instead of removing the finger play characters, point to the appropriate one in the rhyme, or wiggle the appropriate finger to indicate to the children which character you are currently focusing on. You can collectively count the characters as you put them away.

Making the Traditional Finger Play Glove

You'll need:

- fun fur or heavy fabric, pale color
- sewing machine and thread (optionally you can hand-sew the glove)
- scissors
- glue gun
- velcro

You can either enlarge and copy the ambidextrous glove pattern on page 16 to fit your hand (with seam allowance), or you can make your own pattern for a glove by simply tracing your hand onto a piece of paper. Make sure that you allow plenty of seam allowance so that your glove will not be too tight after stitching.

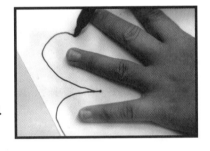

Select a fabric. Gloves made with heavier material such as fun fur tend to be more appealing. Trace the pattern onto the **wrong side** of the material. With right sides together, stitch the glove, leaving an opening for the wrist. Trim and turn. Hem the wrist.

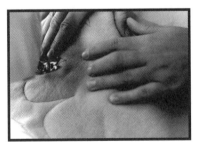

Hand sew six velcro squares to your glove: one for each of the five fingers and one square in the middle of the palm. Alternatively you may glue the velcro on with a high-heat industrial glue gun. **Note:** velcro consists of two distinct strip sides—a hook side and a pile side. It doesn't matter whether you use the hook or pile side

for your glove, but make sure that you use the opposite of what you have selected on the glove for all of your finger play characters and letters.

Quick And Easy Method!

The quick and easy method for making a finger play glove is to purchase a pre-sewn soft dusting or gardening glove and to glue velcro squares to it—one on each finger tip and one in the middle of the palm. This glove does not provide as dramatic a presentation as the sewn glove, but for those who do not sew, it is a reasonable alternative.

Making the Alphabet Letters

You'll Need:

- fun foam

- scissors

- glue gun

- purchased alphabet letters (optional)

- velcro

You can either purchase pre-made alphabet letters in fun foam or plastic, or you can create your own sets of letters with fun foam. If you choose to create your own, enlarge and copy the alphabet patterns on pages 17–18. Select either capital or small letters, but do not mix. Each capital letter should be about 1 ¼" (3.2 cm.) in height. Cut out two of each letter. With a glue gun, glue each letter onto a background piece of fun foam approximately 1 ½"–2" (4–5 cm.) square. Glue velcro to the back of each square, ensuring that the velcro side is the opposite to which you used on the glove.

Making the Finger Play Characters

You'll Need:

- fun foam

- scissors

- glue gun

- an assortment of roly eyes

- fabric paint, various colors (fine-point permanent markers are an alternative)

- other materials as indicated in individual chapters (small scraps of yarn, small chains, pipe cleaners, etc.).
- velcro

The finger play characters are relatively fast and simple to construct, and require only tracing, cutting, and gluing to do so. Each chapter indicates patterns and instructions specific to the character being introduced. Follow the simple instructions for each character. When attaching the velcro to the back of each character, ensure that the velcro side is the opposite to which you used on the glove.

Putting It All Together

Each of the 26 themed chapters that follow are dedicated to a specific letter of the alphabet and a specific character that begins with this letter. An introductory spelling component, along with an alliteration exercise follows. Finger plays, themed book resources, ABC activities, and creative activities are all introduced to create a well-rounded, phonemically aware program for preschoolers.

Following the chapters is a list of alphabet books and a list of relevant and related sources. It is my hope that these suggestions will help you to create varied and exciting storytime programs that lead to early literacy development and future academic success for your young audiences.

Glove Pattern

Enlarge for your hand size.
Allow extra space for seam.

Letters for Glove

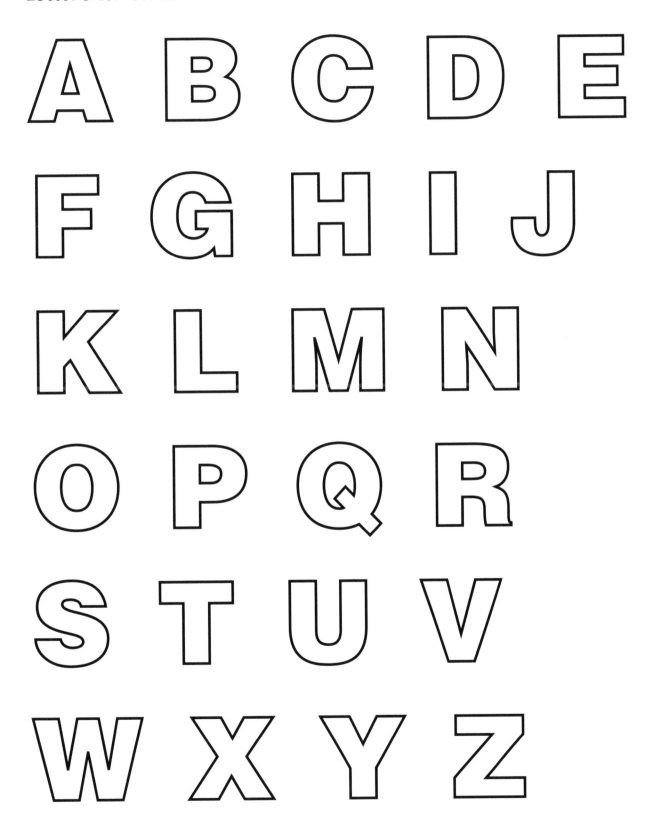

Letters for Glove

A – Apple

Introduction

Apples can be used in storytimes with a variety of themes: food, autumn and harvest, fruits, colors, shapes, and trees or plants. The short "a" sound is a vital one for children to recognize, as it is one of the most popular vowel sounds.

Introductory Poem

It starts with "a" and ends with "ple."
To eat one from a tree you pull.

Finger Play Speller

- Use the finger play glove following the pattern and instructions on pages 13–16.
- Make one each of a, p, p, l, e for the glove using the patterns on pages 17–18.
- Make one apple finger play character using the pattern on page 23.
- Affix the apple finger play character in the center velcro tab of the glove.
- One by one, attach the a, p, p, l, e letters onto the glove. Pause between each one, focusing on the sounds and the blends: a ap app appl apple. Once "apple" has been achieved, spell the word by pointing to the letters and saying them out loud.

Name Game

- Have the children think of the name of a person that begins with "a" (Alice, Adam, Anna, etc.).
- Have children work on sentences that focus on the "a" sound (Alice and Andy ate apples in Ascot. Anna adores all apples. Etc.). Make the sentences as silly as possible.

Finger Plays

- Make five of the apple finger play character using the pattern and instructions on page 23.
- Practice rhyming sounds with the finger plays. Use the ones provided, or look for others. Use the finger play characters to count either up or down with the plays.

Count Down Rhyme

"Five Red Apples" (Sung to the tune "Five Bran Muffins" on *Sidewalk Shuffle*. Sandra Beech. A&M Records, 1984.)

Five red apples on an apple tree.

Five red apples, just as sweet as can be.

A boy came by with a stick one day.

He knocked down an apple, and he ate it right away.

(Repeat for 4, 3, 2, 1)

No red apples on an apple tree.

No red apples just as sweet as can be.

A boy came by with a stick one day.

Sorry little boy, no red apples today.

Count Down Rhyme

"Five Red Apples"

Five red apples, juicy to the core.

Father picked one ... CRUNCH, CRUNCH!

And then there were four.

Four red apples, high up in a tree.

Mother picked one ... CRUNCH, CRUNCH!

And then there were three.

Three red apples, looking down at you.

Brother picked one ... CRUNCH, CRUNCH!

And then there were two.

Two red apples, hanging in the sun.

Sister picked one ... CRUNCH, CRUNCH!

And then there was one.

One red apple fell down to the lawn.

I ate it ... CRUNCH, CRUNCH!

And now they are all gone.

(As an alternative to family members, substitute names of children in program.)

Resources for Storytime

Use some of these books and poems, or any of your favorites, to create a well-rounded storytime program.

Books

Atwood, Margaret. *Up in the Tree.* Groundwood, 2006. Two children have fun in an apple tree.

Benjamin, A. H., and Gwyneth Williamson. *Little Mouse and the Big Red Apple.* Scholastic, 2002. A hungry mouse, struggling to bring home a big apple, doesn't want to share with the animals who help along the way.

Bosca, Francesca. *The Apple King.* Illustrated by Giuliano Ferri. North-South Books, 2001. A selfish King keeps a beautiful apple tree to himself, until an invasion of worms teaches him a lesson about sharing.

Bunting, Eve. *One Green Apple.* Illustrated by Ted Lewin. Clarion Books, 2006. A young immigrant gains self-confidence when she picks a green apple that compliments the other red apples her classmates have picked while on a school trip.

Gibbons, Gail. *The Seasons of Arnold's Apple Tree.* Harcourt, 2001. As the seasons pass, Arnold enjoys a variety of activities with his apple tree.

Hubbell, Will. *Apples Here.* Albert Whitman, 2002. Through the seasons, apples grow from buds to blossoms to fruit and become part of people's lives and celebrations.

Kleven, Elisa. *The Apple Doll.* Farrar, Straus and Giroux, 2007. Apprehensive about starting school, Lizzy makes a doll out of an apple from her favorite tree to take with her to school. Includes apple doll instructions.

Lear, Edward. *A Was Once an Apple Pie.* Illustrated by Suse MacDonald. Orchard Books, 2005. Lively illustrations bring Lear's well-known poem to life.

Mayer, Mercer. *Harvest Time.* McGraw-Hill, 2004. Little Critter and his younger sister help their grandparents pick pumpkins and apples.

Miller, Virginia. *Ten Red Apples.* Candlewick Press, 2002. Bartholomew and George, two bears, and little Kitten enjoy the apple tree and count the shiny red apples.

Nidey, Kelli. *When Autumn Falls.* Illustrated by Susan Swan. Albert Whitman, 2004. Observes the fall season with falling leaves and apples.

Noble, Trinka Hakes. *Apple Tree Christmas.* Sleeping Bear Press, 2005. When their apple tree is felled by a storm just before Christmas, a young farm girl and her family discover the importance the tree had for all of them.

Purmell, Ann. *Apple Cider Making Days.* Illustrated by Joanne Friar. Millbrook Press, 2002. Alex and Abigail join the whole family in processing and selling apples and cider at their grandfather's farm.

Ruelle, Karen Gray. *Easy as Apple Pie.* Holiday House, 2002. Emily says "yuck" to apples, but thinks differently when she and her brother make apple pies at their grandparents' house.

Shapiro, Jody Fickes. *Up, Up, Up! It's Apple-picking Time.* Illustrated by Kitty Harvill. Scholastic, 2003. Myles and his family go to his grandparents' apple ranch where they have a wonderful time picking and selling apples together.

Wallace, Nancy Elizabeth. *Apples, Apples, Apples.* Scholastic, 2000. Members of the Rabbit family visit an apple orchard where they have fun picking apples and discovering their many uses.

Wellington, Monica. *Apple Farmer Annie.* Puffin, 2004. Annie the apple farmer saves her most beautiful apples to sell at the farmer's market.

Winget, Susan. *Tucker's Apple-Dandy Day.* HarperCollins, 2006. Tucker the rabbit goes on a class trip to Farmer Sam's apple orchard.

Poems

"Way up High in an Apple Tree"
(Traditional)
Way up high in an apple tree,

A great big apple looked down at me.

I shook that tree as hard as I could.

Down came the apple, and Mmmm, was it good!

(Have children act out activities, looking up, shaking tree, sampling apple.)

"Here's My Little Apple Tree"

Here's my little apple tree, (*Spread fingers on one hand to make tree.*)

With lovely leaves so green.

Here's my pretty apples, (*Circle hands together to form shape of apple.*)

With a red and glossy sheen.

When autumn weather comes around,

My apples soon will fall. (*Pat knees with fists, imitating apples falling.*)

I take an apple basket, (*Circle arms to form a basket.*)

And I gather up them all. (*Pretend to place apples in the basket.*)

"A Was an Apple Pie" (This is an old alphabet rhyme that can be found in book format, or look on the Internet for it.)

Alphabet Activities

ABC Connect-the-Dots

Copy one pattern on page 24 for each child. Have the children connect the dots from A to Z to find the mystery picture.

Apple Tree Alphabet

Enlarge and copy one each of the patterns on pages 25–26 for each child. Have the children color the tree and the apples and cut out the apples. The children can match the alphabet apples to the appropriate spot on the tree then glue them in place.

Creative Activities

Fingerprint Apple Tree

Have the children draw and color a tree onto construction or finger paint paper. Using red finger paint, have the children press apple fingerprints on the tree.

Apple Prints

Apples sliced horizontally through the middle create an interesting print when used with tempera paint. The apple core creates a star effect.

Apple Display

Have a variety of different types of apples on hand. Discuss the different shapes, colors, and sizes of apples. Samples of different apples could be provided.

Apple Treats

A number of apple recipes are available for cookies, squares, and cakes. Make a few treats for the children.

Creating Apple Characters

Make five apples.

- Trace apple pattern onto red fun foam.
- Trace leaf pattern onto green fun foam.
- Trace stem pattern onto brown fun foam.
- Cut out all the pieces.
- Glue one stem and leaf to each apple.
- Glue velcro to back.

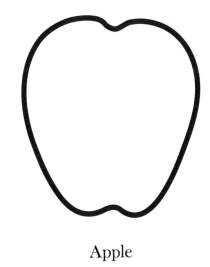

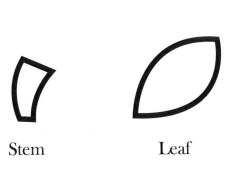

Stem   Leaf

Apple

_pple

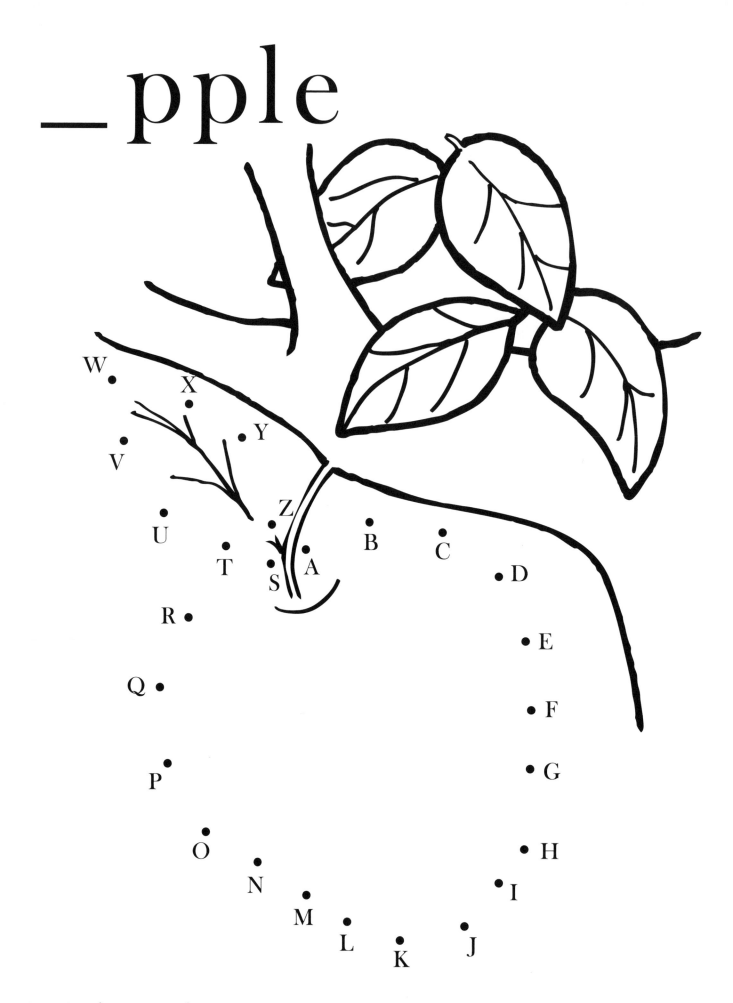

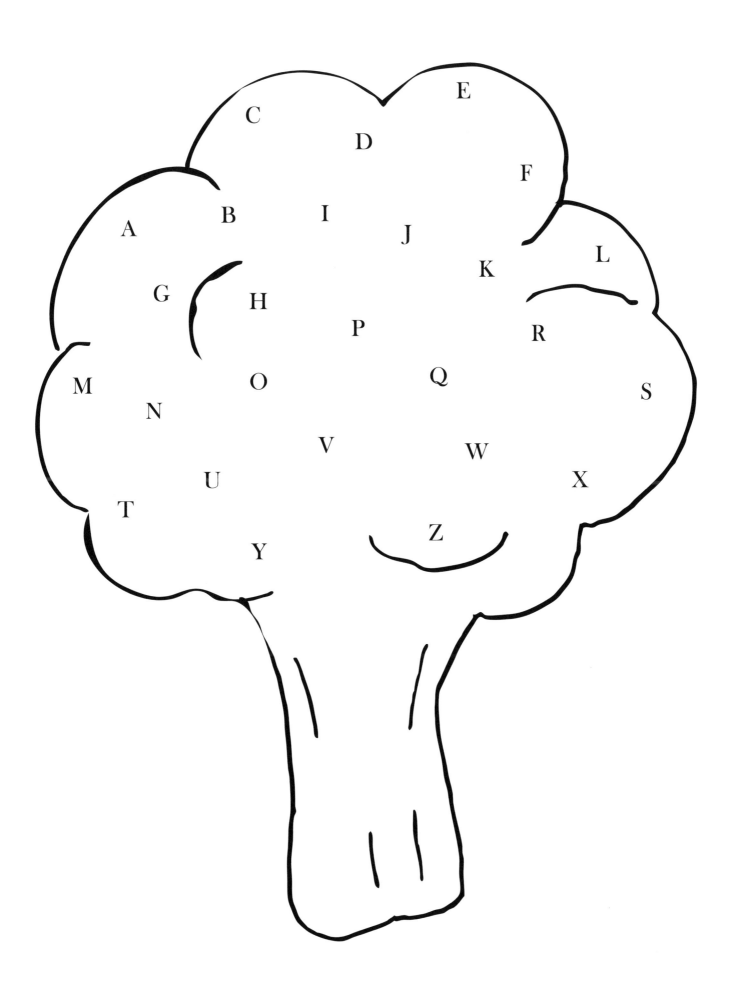

Apple Patterns

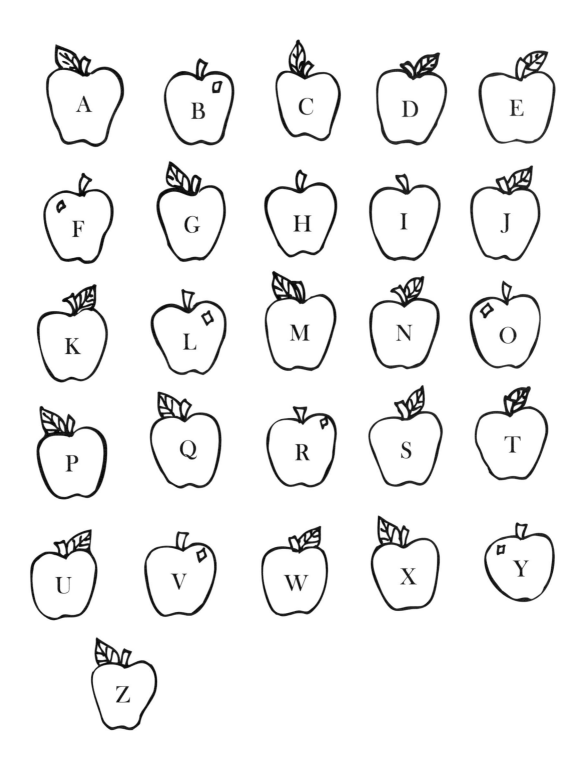

A A A A A A A A A A A

A - - - - - - - - - - - - A

a a a a a a a a a a a a

a - - - - - - - - - - - - a

Aa Aa Aa Aa Aa Aa

Aa - - - - - - - - - - - Aa

B — Bird

Introduction

This is truly a program that can be conducted at any time of the year. In the Spring, the focus is on eggs and baby birds. A Summer program is equally suitable, as birds are most visible at this time. In the Autumn, many birds get ready to migrate south—hence another theme, and in the winter the focus could be on bird feeders. The "b" sound requires a lot of practice to master, and to distinguish clearly from the "p" sound.

Introductory Poem

She starts with "b" and ends with "ird." From her a "tweet, tweet" sound is heard.

Finger Play Speller

- Use the finger play glove following the pattern and instructions on pages 13–16.
- Make one each of b, i, r, d for the glove using the patterns on pages 17–18.

- Make one bird finger play character using the pattern on page 32.
- Affix the bird finger play character in the center velcro tab of the glove.
- One by one, attach the b, i, r, d letters onto the glove. Pause between each one, focusing on the sounds and the blends: b bi bir bird. Once "bird" has been achieved, spell the word by pointing to the letters and saying them out loud.

Name Game

- Have the children think of the name of a person that begins with "b" (Bob, Betty, Brenda, etc.).
- Have children work on sentences that focus on the "b" sound (Betty the bird buys beach balls. Bob the boxer builds birdhouses. Etc.). Make the sentences as silly as possible.

Finger Plays

- Make five of the bird finger play character using the pattern and instructions on page 32.

- Practice rhyming sounds with the finger plays. Use the ones provided, or look for others. Use the finger play characters to count either up or down with the plays.

Stay and Play Rhyme

"Five Baby Birds" (Traditional)

Five baby birds, in a nest in a tree
are just as hungry as they can be.

"Peep," said baby bird number one, "Mother said she soon would come."

"Peep, peep," said baby bird number two, "If she doesn't come, what will we do?"

"Peep, peep, peep," said baby bird number three, "I hope that she can find our tree."

"Peep, peep, peep, peep," said baby four, "She never was this late before."

"Peep, peep, peep, peep, peep," said number five, "When will our mother bird arrive?"

Well here she comes they soon can see, and they're as happy as can be.

Count Up Rhyme

"One Little Bird"

There was one little bird who lived up in a tree.

He was all alone, and he didn't want to be.

So he flew far away, over the big blue sea.

And he brought back a friend to live in the tree.

(Repeat for 2, 3, 4)

Resources for Storytime

Use some of these books and poems, or any of your favorites, to create a well-rounded storytime program.

Books

Collard III, Sneed B. *Beaks!* Illustrated by Robin Brickman. Charlesbridge, 2002. Simple text and 3D paper-sculpted illustrations describe various bird beaks and how birds use them.

Crowther, Kitty. *Jack & Jim.* Hyperion Books for Children, 2000. A blackbird and a seagull become friends.

DePalma, Mary Newell. *The Strange Egg.* Houghton Mifflin, 2001. A little bird tries to hatch a strange egg before a monkey tells her it is an orange.

DiPucchio, Kelly. *What's the Magic Word?* HarperCollins, 2005. A newly hatched bird tries to find a home by using different animal passwords.

Franco, Betsy. *Bird Songs.* Illustrated by Steve Jenkins. Margaret K. McElderry Books, 2007. Birds sing from day to night, beginning with the woodpecker who taps ten times and counting down to the hummingbird who calls once.

George, Jean Craighead. *Luck.* Illustrated by Wendell Minor. Laura Geringer Books, 2006. A young sandhill crane finds his place in the crane migration from Canada to the Platte River.

Gerstein, Mordicai. *Sparrow Jack.* Farrar/Frances Foster Books, 2003. The story of a man who brought sparrows to America in the 1860s.

Haas, Irene. *Bess and Bella.* Margaret K. McElderry Books, 2006. Bess is feeling terribly lonely when a bird named Bella suddenly appears with a tiny suitcase full of wonderful surprises.

James, Simon. *The Birdwatchers.* Candlewick Press, 2002. A young girl accompanies her grandfather on a bird-watching expedition.

Keller, Holly. *Sophie's Window.* Greenwillow Books, 2005. When a little bird who is afraid to fly is blown out of his home, he must rely on a new friend to take him back to his parents.

Lester, Helen. *Princess Penelope's Parrot.* Illustrated by Lynn Munsinger. Walter Lorraine Books, 2001. The Princess cannot get her parrot to talk, except in embarrassing circumstances.

Minshull, Evelyn. *Eaglet's World.* Illustrated by Andrea Gabriel. Albert Whitman, 2002. A young eaglet hesitates to leave the comfort of his parents' nest.

Napoli, Donna Jo. *Albert.* Illustrated by Jim LaMarche. Silver Whistle/Harcourt Brace, 2001. Two cardinals come to build a nest in Albert's hand.

Newman, Marjorie. *Mole and the Baby Bird.* Illustrated by Patrick Benson. Bloomsbury Children's Books, 2004. Mole rescues a baby bird and cares for it, but realizes that he must set it free.

Rockwell, Anne. *Two Blue Jays.* Illustrated by Megan Halsey. Walker & Co., 2003. A classroom of children get a front-row view as a pair of blue jays build a nest.

Schwartz, Ellen. *Abby's Birds.* Illustrated by Sima Elizabeth Shefrin. Tradewind Books, 2006. Abby moves to a new house and makes friends with her Japanese neighbor who shares her love of the robins that nest in her garden. Includes origami instructions.

St. Pierre, Stephanie. *What the Sea Saw.* Illustrated by Beverly Doyle. Peachtree Publishers, 2006. A lyrical introduction to the sea, its inhabitants, and its role in the world around it. Includes facts about the ecosystems of oceans and shorelines.

Tafuri, Nancy. *Whose Chick Are You?* Greenwillow Books, 2007. Goose, Duck,

Hen, Bird, and the little chick itself cannot tell to whom a new hatchling belongs.

Poems

Kiesler, Kate, ed. *Wings on the Wind: Bird Poems*. Clarion, 2002.

"Lovebirds" in *Bear Hugs: Romantically Ridiculous Animal Rhymes* by Karma Wilson. Margaret K. McElderry Books, 2005.

"One Old Owl" in *The Frogs Wore Red Suspenders* by Jack Prelutsky. Illustrated by Petra Mathers. Greenwillow, 2002.

"Penguins" in *The Llama Who Had No Pajama: 100 Favorite Poems* by Mary Ann Hoberman. Illustrated by Betty Fraser. Harcourt, 2006.

"Singing Birds" in *Seasons: A Book of Poems* by Charlotte Zolotow. Illustrated by Erik Blegvad. HarperTrophy, 2002.

"Snowbirds" in *See Saw Saskatchewan: More Playful Poems from Coast to Coast* by Robert Heidbreder. Illustrated by Scot Ritchie. Kids Can Press, 2003.

"Spring Madness" in *Give Yourself to the Rain: Poems for the Very Young*. Margaret Wise Brown. Illustrated by Teri L. Weidner. Margaret K. McElderry Books, 2002.

"Yellowthroat" in *Exploding Gravy: Poems to Make You Laugh*. X. J. Kennedy.

Illustrated by Joy Allen. Little, Brown and Company, 2002.

"Two Little Dickie Birds" (Traditional)
Two little dickie birds, sitting on a hill—
One named Jack, the other named Jill.
Fly away Jack, fly away Jill,
Come back Jack, come back Jill.

Note: Generally this is done with the index fingers of each hand extended. When Jack and Jill "fly away," the hands are moved to behind the back. When Jack and Jill "come back," the hands are brought forward again.

Alphabet Activities

ABC Connect-the-Dots

Copy one pattern on page 33 for each child. Have the children connect the dots from A to Z to find the mystery picture.

Bird Feeder Alphabet

Enlarge and copy one each of the patterns on pages 34–35 for each child. Have the children color the bird feeder and the birds and cut out the birds. The children can match the alphabet birds to the appropriate spot on the bird feeder, then glue them in place.

Creative Activities

Bird Feeders

Have children make their own bird feeders to take home. There are many examples of bird feeders in craft books, but a simple one is to roll a pine cone first in peanut butter, then bird seed. Be sure to attach a piece of string to the pine cone before rolling. Ensure that no children have peanut allergies before trying this craft.

Bird Calls

There are a number of nature tapes that have songs of wild birds on them. Play some of the different bird calls and have children guess which bird is singing. Use easy ones like robin, blue jay, chickadee, and crow.

Bird Feathers

Collect a few varieties of bird feathers. Make sure they are clean, and ensure no children have allergies to feathers.

Discuss the length, shape, and structure of the feathers. Children may identify which birds the feathers come from.

Follow the Flying Leader

Have the children pretend that they are a flock of birds. The lead bird flies, flaps his wings, twists and dives, and the other children imitate the leader. Alternate leaders.

Creating Bird Characters

Make five birds.

- Trace bird and wing patterns onto blue fun foam.
- Trace face pattern onto white fun foam.
- Trace beak pattern onto yellow fun foam.
- Cut out all the pieces.
- Glue one face and beak to each bird.
- Glue wing to body.
- Glue medium-size roly eye on.
- Glue velcro to back.

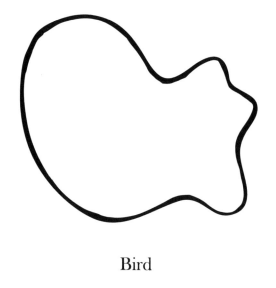

Bird

Beak

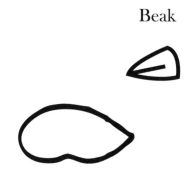

Wing

Face

_ird

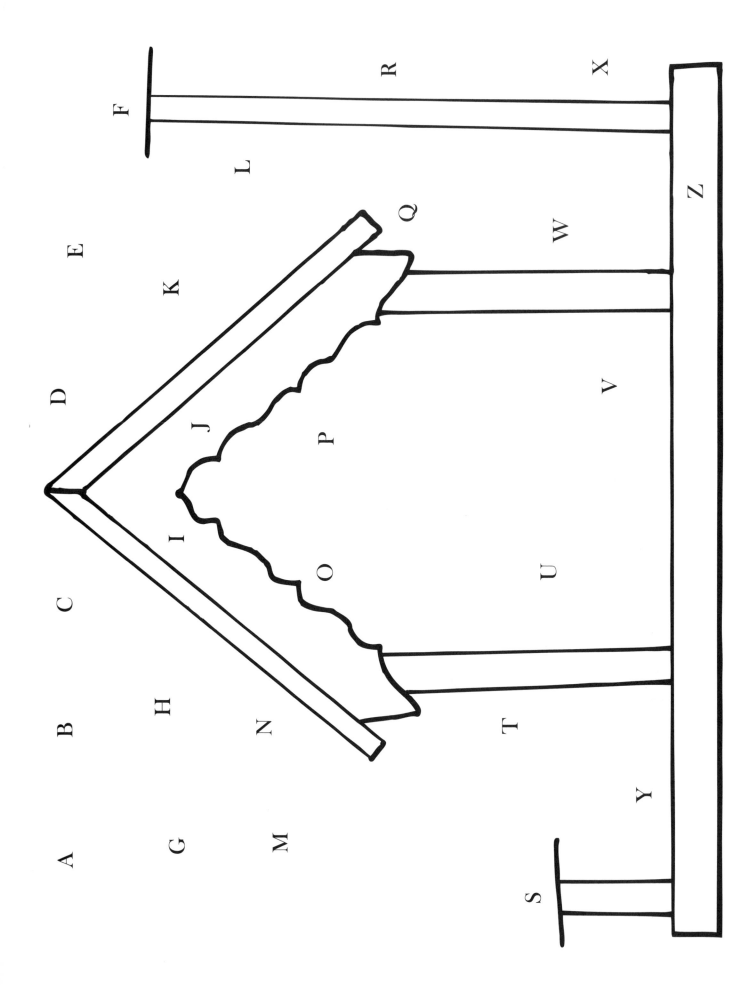

Bird Patterns

B B B B B B B B B B B

B B

b b b b b b b b b b b

b b

Bb Bb Bb Bb Bb Bb

Bb Bb

C — Cow

Introduction

Every child loves imitating animal sounds, and the cow ranks high on their list of preferences. Cows can be applied to themes of animals, farms, food, and sounds and can be used in any season. The hard "c" sound is a useful one for children to practice.

Introductory Poem

She starts with "c" and ends with "ow."
She says "moo, moo," though we don't know how.

Finger Play Speller

- Use the finger play glove following the pattern and instructions on pages 13–16.

- Make one each of c, o, w for the glove using the patterns on pages 17–18.

- Make one cow finger play character using the pattern on page 41.

- Affix the cow finger play character in the center velcro tab of the glove.

- One by one, attach the c, o, w letters onto the glove. Pause between each one, focusing on the sounds and the blends: c co cow. Once "cow" has been achieved, spell the word by pointing to the letters and saying them out loud.

Name Game

- Have the children think of the name of a person that begins with "c" (Clara, Cameron, Carla, etc.).

- Have children work on sentences that focus on the "c" sound (Clara the cow chews cakes and candy. Cameron calls cows to come closer. Etc.). Make the sentences as silly as possible.

Finger Plays

- Make five of the cow finger play character, using the pattern and instructions on pages 40–41.

- Practice rhyming sounds with the finger plays. Use the ones provided, or look for others. Use the finger play characters to count either up or down with the plays.

Count Down Rhyme

"Five Little Cows" (Sung to the tune "Camptown Races.")

Five little cows ate grass all day.

Moo-moo, moo-moo,

Grazing in the fields of hay.

Moo-moo-moo-moo,

They ate and ate their fill.

They ate and ate until

One little cow had enough that day …

And slowly walked away.

(Repeat for 4, 3, 2, 1)

Stay and Play Rhyme

"This Little Cow" (Adapted from Traditional)

This little cow chewed the sweet long hay.

This little cow roamed the fields all day.

This little cow found a nice shady spot.

This little cow found the fields too hot.

This little cow said, "Moo, moo, moo—

The farmer has some milking to do."

Resources for Storytime

Use some of these books and poems, or any of your favorites, to create a well-rounded storytime program.

Books

Barroux. *Where's Mary's Hat?* Viking, 2003. Mary the cow asks all the animals if they have seen her hat. No one has seen it—until she asks bear, who hasn't seen her hat but has a new kite.

Cazet, Denys. *Minnie and Moo and the Haunted Sweater.* HarperCollins, 2007. Minnie and Moo want to give special presents to the farmer for his birthday, but something goes wrong when Moo knits him a sweater. See others in the "Minnie and Moo" series of beginning readers.

Cronin, Doreen. *Click, Clack, Moo: Cows that Type.* Illustrated by Betsy Lewin. Simon & Schuster Books for Young Readers, 2000. Farmer Brown's cows discover a typewriter in the barn and start making demands.

Cronin, Doreen. *Dooby Dooby Moo.* Illustrated by Betsy Lewin. Atheneum Books for Young Readers, 2006. While Farmer Brown sleeps, his animals prepare for a talent show.

Fajerman, Deborah. *How to Speak Moo!* Random House Children's Books, 2002. All cows say is "moo," but how they say it means a lot.

Fleming, Denise. *The Cow Who Clucked.* Henry Holt & Company, 2006. When a cow loses her moo, she searches to see if another animal in the barn has it.

Fox, Mem. *A Particular Cow*. Illustrated by Terry Denton. Harcourt, 2006. A particular cow has some particularly strange adventures on a particular day.

Freeman, Martha. *Mrs. Wow Never Wanted a Cow*. Illustrated by Steven Salerno. Random House, 2006. When Mrs. Wow takes in a stray cow, her lazy dog and cat hope to train the new household member. (A Beginning Reader.)

Hurd, Thacher. *Moo Cow Kaboom!* HarperCollins, 2003. A romp to space and back with an abducted cow and some aliens.

Maar, Paul. *Gloria the Cow*. Illustrated by Tina Schulte. Translated by Alexis L. Spry. NorthSouth Books, 2006. Gloria dreams big, but in order to become a star, she must take her act on the road.

Milgrim, David. *Cows Can't Fly*. Puffin, 2000. A child tries to convince others that cows can fly when a drawing of one is blown away by a breeze.

Moody, Camilla. *Millie Moo: Follow Millie on Her Wacky Farmyard Adventure!* St. Martin's Press, 2005. Help Millie Moo find her farmyard friends in this wacky touch and feel picture book, packed with crazy characters, funny rhymes, and lots to find and do!

Palatini, Margie. *Moo Who?* Illustrated by Keith Graves. HarperCollins, 2004. After being hit on the head, Hilda the singing cow forgets what sound she makes.

Root, Phyllis. *Kiss the Cow*. Illustrated by Will Hillenbrand. Candlewick Press, 2000. The family cow is upset when Annalisa refuses to kiss it before milking it.

Silverman, Erica. *Cowgirl Kate and Cocoa*. Illustrated by Betsy Lewin. Harcourt, 2005. Cowgirl Kate and her hungry cow horse Cocoa count cows, share a story, and help each other fall asleep.

Spinelli, Eileen. *Something to Tell the Grandcows*. Illustrated by Bill Slavin. Eerdman Books, 2004. A cow who is bored with her ordinary life joins an expedition to the south pole.

Wheeler, Lisa. *Sixteen Cows*. Illustrated by Kurt Cyrus. Harcourt, 2002. The cows of neighboring ranches get mixed up in a storm.

Poems

"Bossy Cow" in *MaMa Goose: Rhymes and Poems for the Little Ones.* by Edelen Willie. Andrews McMeel Publishing, 2003.

"The Cow" in *The Children's Treasury: Fairy Tales, Nursery Rhymes and Nonsense Verse.* Alice Mills, ed. Whitecap Books, 2002.

"Cow and Calf" in *Wake Up, Sleepy Head!: Early Morning Poems*. Illustrated by Dubravka Kolanovic. Child's Play, 2004.

"Cows." in *Exploding Gravy: Poems to Make You Laugh*. X. J. Kennedy. Illustrated by Joy Allen. Little, Brown and Company, 2002.

"Cows in the Kitchen" in *Oh My Darling, Porcupine and other Silly Sing-Along Songs*. Illustrated by Stephen Carpenter. Meadowbrook Press, 2006.

Alphabet Activities

ABC Connect-the-Dots

Copy one pattern on page 42 for each child. Have the children connect the dots from A to Z to find the mystery picture.

Cow Alphabet

Enlarge and copy one each of the patterns on pages 43–44 for each child. Have the children cut out the individual pieces of the cow. The children can match the alphabet cow pieces to the appropriate spot on the cow picture then glue them in place.

Creative Activities

A Calf Is Born

A number of nonfiction books show pictures of new calves and the birthing process. Show some of these pictures and discuss with children.

Milk Products

Explain to the children about milking cows and have a variety of milk products on hand for the children to sample, i.e.: milk, yogurt, cheese, ice cream.

Milking the Cow

Have children pretend that they are milking a cow. You may choose to include a song about milking.

Creating Cow Characters

Make five cows.

- Trace cow pattern from page 41 onto white fun foam.
- Trace udder and muzzle patterns onto pink fun foam.
- Trace spots pattern onto black fun foam.
- Cut out all the pieces.
- Glue spots, muzzle, and udder onto cow. Make each cow a little different by varying the spot sizes and locations.
- Glue small roly eyes on.
- Paint nostrils on muzzle using pink fabric paint.
- Braid three small pieces of black and white yarn. Tie top and bottom. Glue onto cow for tail.
- Glue velcro to back.

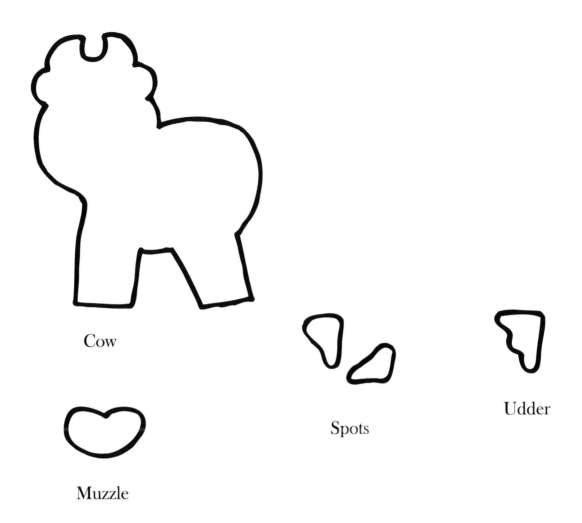

Cow

Muzzle

Spots

Udder

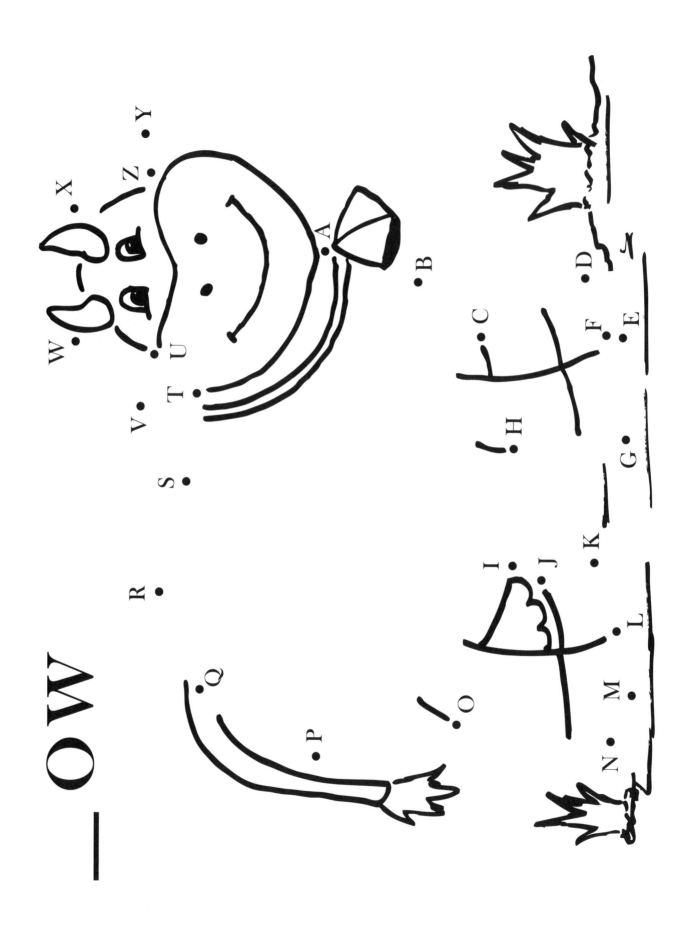

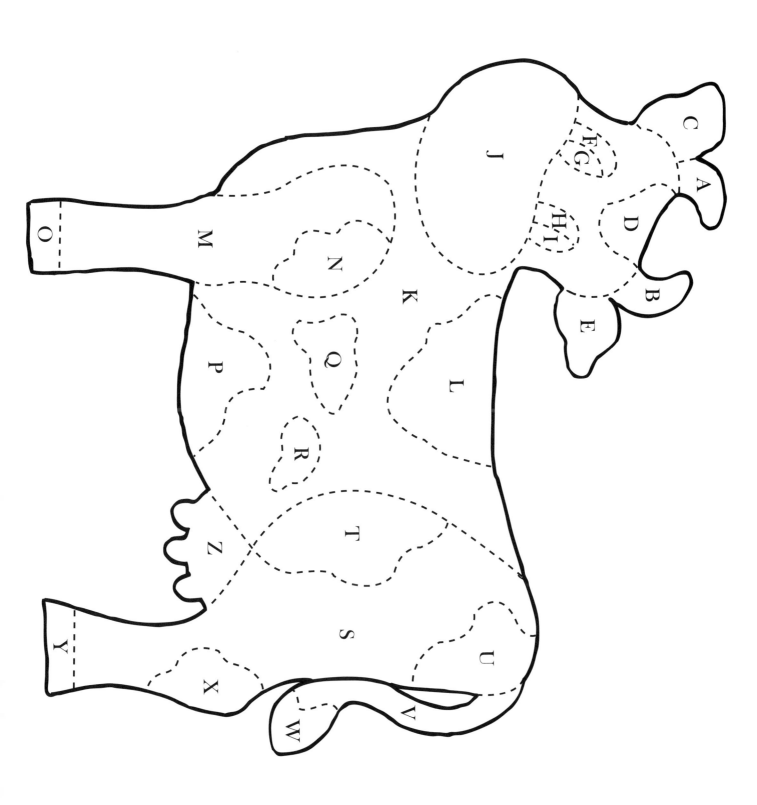

Cow Pattern

C C C C C C C C C C

C — — — — — — — — — C

C C C C C C C C C C C

C — — — — — — — — — C

Cc Cc Cc Cc Cc Cc

Cc — — — — — — — Cc

D — Duck

Introduction

This is another very popular topic for storytime. It is adaptable for themes of birds, rainy days, farms, and farm animals, and it also stands alone as a theme. Encourage children to make the "d" sound fairly short, so as not to say "duh."

Introductory Poem

She starts with "d" and ends with "uck." She says "quack, quack" in water and muck.

Finger Play Speller

- Use the finger play glove following the pattern and instructions on pages 13–16.

- Make one each of d, u, c, k for the glove using the patterns on pages 17–18.

- Make one duck finger play character using the pattern on page 50.

- Affix the duck finger play character in the center velcro tab of the glove.

- One by one, attach the d, u, c, k letters onto the glove. Pause between each one, focusing on the sounds and the blends: d du duc duck. Once "duck" has been achieved, spell the word by pointing to the letters and saying them out loud.

Name Game

- Have the children think of the name of a person that begins with "d" (Daniel, Dora, Drew, etc.).

- Have children work on sentences that focus on the "d" sound (Daniel the duck dips all day. Dora duck dawdles during dinner. Etc.). Make the sentences as silly as possible.

Finger Plays

- Make five of the duck finger play character using the pattern and instructions on page 50.

- Practice rhyming sounds with the finger plays. Use the ones provided, or look for others. Use the finger play characters to count either up or down with the plays.

Count Down Rhyme

"Five Little Ducks" (Traditional)

Five little ducks went swimming one day

Over the hills and far away.

Mother duck said, "Quack, quack, quack."

But only four little ducks came back.

(**End of "one" duck line:** But NO little ducks came waddling back.)

(Repeat for 4, 3, 2, 1)

Sad Mother duck went swimming one day

Over the hills and far away.

Mother duck said, "Quack, quack, quack."

And five little ducks came swimming back.

Count Up Rhyme

"One Little Duck"

One little duck in the pond so blue

Called for a friend ... QUACK!

And then there were two.

Two little ducks, swimming 'round with glee

Called for a friend ... QUACK, QUACK!

And then there were three.

Three little ducks, paddling near the shore

Called for a friend ... QUACK, QUACK, QUACK!

And then there were four.

Four little ducks, learning how to dive

Called for a friend ... QUACK, QUACK, QUACK, QUACK!

And then there were five.

Five little ducks near the end of the day

Hear the hunters coming ...

And they all swam away.

Also try "Three Loud Ducks" in *Animal Piggyback Songs.* Edited by Gayle Bittinger. Warren Publishing House, 1990. (Adapt to five loud ducks for use with the fingerplay characters.)

Resources for Storytime

Use some of these books and poems, or any of your favorites, to create a well-rounded storytime program.

Books

Alborough, Jez. *Hit the Ball, Duck.* HarperCollins, 2005. A little duck learns to play baseball.

Aruego, José, and Ariane Dewey. *The Last Laugh.* Dial Books for Young Readers, 2006. A wordless tale in which a clever duck outwits a bullying snake.

Asch, Frank. *Baby Duck's New Friend.* Harcourt, 2001. Baby Duck wanders away from home, not realizing that he must find his way back.

Berry, Lynne. *Duck Skates.* Illustrated by Hiroe Nakata. Henry Holt & Company, 2005. Five little ducks skate, romp, and play in the snow.

Buzzeo, Toni. *Dawdle Duckling.* Illustrated by Margaret Spengler. Puffin, 2005. Mama Duck tries to keep Dawdle Duckling together with his siblings.

Cronin, Doreen. *Giggle, Giggle, Quack.* Illustrated by Betsy Lewin. Simon & Schuster Books for Young Readers, 2002. Duck makes trouble for Farmer Brown's brother when he is left in charge of the farm. A sequel to *Click, Clack, Moo.*

Ford, Bernette G. *No More Diapers for Ducky!* Illustrated by Sam Williams. Boxer Books, 2006. When Piggy can't come out to play because he is using the potty, Ducky decides it's time for him to learn to use the potty too.

Hills, Tad. *Duck & Goose.* Schwartz & Wade Books, 2006. Duck and Goose learn to work together to take care of a ball, which they think is an egg.

Hindley, Judy. *Do Like a Duck Does.* Illustrated by Ivan Bates. Candlewick Press, 2002. A mother duck challenges a stranger to imitate a duck's behavior and proves that he is a fox.

Johansen, Hanna. *The Duck and the Owl.* Illustrated by Kathi Bhend. David R. Goodine, 2005. A duck and an owl consider becoming friends, despite their differences in appearance and behavior.

Kaldor, Connie. *A Duck in New York City.* Illustrated by Fil & Julie. The Secret Mountain, 2005. A prairie duck wants to fly to New York City to dance on Broadway. Includes CD.

Long, Ethan. *Tickle the Duck!* Little, Brown and Company, 2006. A cranky duck dares children to tickle him. A touch-and-feel book.

Meyrick, Judith. *Gracie, the Public Gardens Duck.* Illustrated by Richard Rudnicki. Nimbus, 2007. Gracie loves her life at the public gardens, until the regular visitors stop feeding her. What's a duck to do?

Peters, Lisa Westberg. *Cold Little Duck, Duck, Duck.* Illustrated by Sam Williams. HarperFestival, 2005. Early one spring a little duck arrives at her pond and finds it still frozen.

Skalak, Barbara Anne. *Waddle, Waddle, Quack, Quack, Quack.* Illustrated by Sylvia Long. Chronicle Books, 2005. A little duckling gets separated from the rest of the family while out exploring.

Tafuri, Nancy. *Goodnight, My Duckling.*

Scholastic, 2006. As a mother duck leads her ducklings home, one dawdles and is left behind.

Thompson, Lauren. *Little Quack's New Friend.* Illustrated by Derek Anderson. Simon & Schuster, 2006. When a frog invites five ducklings to play, all but Little Quack decline. See also *Little Quack.*

Waddell, Martin. *It's Quacking Time.* Illustrated by Jill Barton. Candlewick Press, 2005. Who is coming out of the new egg? See also *Webster J. Duck.*

Poems

"Ducks" in *The Llama Who Had No Pajama* by Mary Ann Hoberman. Illustrated by Betty Fraser. Harcourt, 2006.

"I'm a Yellow-Bill Duck" in *Ride a Purple Pelican* by Jack Prelutsky. Pictures by Garth Williams. Greenwillow Books, 1986.

"When a Yellow Duck" in *1001 Rhymes and Fingerplays for Working with Young Children* compiled by Totline Staff. Edited by Gayle Bittinger et. al. Warren Publishing House, 1994.

Alphabet Activities

ABC Connect-the-Dots

Copy one pattern on page 51 for each child. Have the children connect the dots from A to Z to find the mystery picture.

ABC Duck

Enlarge and copy one of each pattern on pages 52–53 for each child. Have the children cut out the pieces on page 53. Glue pieces onto the appropriate place on duck picture.

Creative Activities

Duck Hats

Enlarge and copy one duck hat pattern from page 50 for each child. Have the children color in the duck picture. Using yellow construction paper, make a band big enough to go around a child's head. Staple to form a ring. Glue on duck face and bill.

Ducks Hatching

A number of nonfiction books show pictures of the development of a duck, from egg to hatching. Children enjoy viewing these types of pictures.

Duck Craft

Cut one segment from an egg carton for each child. Have children glue large yellow pompoms in carton pieces. Next have children glue on bills made from orange felt and roly eyes.

Creating Duck Characters

Make five ducks.

- Trace duck and wing patterns onto yellow fun foam.
- Trace bill pattern onto orange fun foam.
- Cut out all the pieces.
- Glue wing and bill onto duck.
- Glue on large roly eye.
- Glue velcro to back.

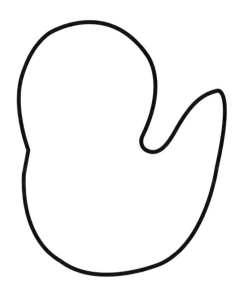

Duck

Wing

Bill

Duck Hat Pattern

_uck

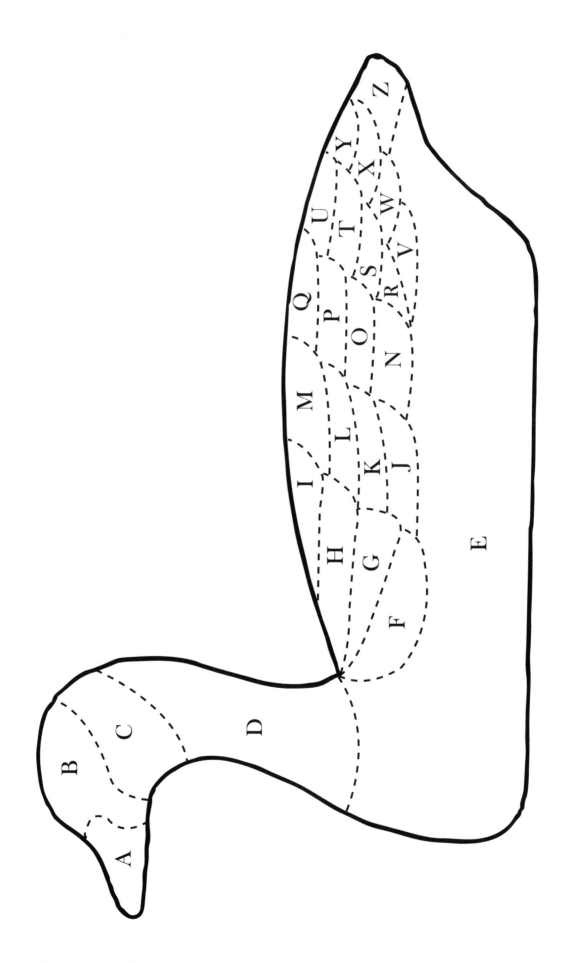

Duck Pattern

D D D D D D D D D D D

D - D

d d d d d d d d d d d d

d - d

Dd Dd Dd Dd Dd

Dd - - - - - - - - - - - - - - - - - - Dd

E — Egg

Introduction

A well-known food to most children, eggs can be incorporated into several themes and seasons. The soft "e" sound is widely used.

Introductory Poem

It starts with "e" and ends with "g."
Chickens lay them near their leg.

Finger Play Speller

- Use the finger play glove following the pattern and instructions on pages 13–16.
- Make one each of e, g, g for the glove using the patterns on pages 17–18.
- Make one egg finger play character using the pattern on page 59.
- Affix the egg finger play character in the center velcro tab of the glove.
- One by one, attach the e, g, g letters onto the glove. Pause between each one, focusing on the sounds and the blends: e eg egg. Once "egg"

has been achieved, spell the word by pointing to the letters and saying them out loud.

Name Game

- Have the children think of the name of a person that begins with "e" (Edna, Elvis, Edward, etc.).
- Have children work on sentences that focus on the "e" sound (Edna lays eggs on every edge. Edward enjoys eggs every day. Etc.). Make the sentences as silly as possible.

Finger Plays

- Make five of the egg finger play character using the pattern and instructions on page 59.
- Practice rhyming sounds with the finger plays. Use the ones provided, or look for others. Use the finger play characters to count either up or down with the plays.

Count Down Rhyme

"Five Little Eggs"

(Sung to the tune "Five Green and Speckled Frogs" on *Singable Songs for the Very Young*. Raffi. Troubadour Records, 1976.)

Five little eggs, you see.

Some for you and some for me.

Waiting for morning to arrive.

One cracked, then opened wide.

And there was a chick inside.

Then there were four eggs left to see.

(Repeat for 4, 3, 2, 1)

You can change the words to *Five Easter Eggs* if doing an Easter theme.

Count Down Rhyme

"Five Little Easter Eggs" (Adapted from Traditional)

Five little Easter eggs, pretty colors wore.

A boy ate the blue one, and then there were four.

Four little Easter eggs, two and two you see.

A girl ate the red one, and then there were three.

Three little Easter eggs, and before I knew—

A boy ate the yellow one, and then there were two.

Two little Easter eggs, oh my what fun.

A girl ate the purple one, and then there was one.

One little Easter egg, all the rest were gone.

I ate the last one, and now there are none.

Resources for Storytime

Use some of these books and poems, or any of your favorites, to create a well-rounded storytime program.

Books

Bunting, Eve. *Hurry! Hurry!* Illustrated by Jeff Mack. Harcourt, 2007. All the animals of the barnyard community hurry to greet their newest member, who is just pecking his way out of an egg.

Burg, Sarah. *One More Egg*. North-South Books, 2006. A rabbit, who asks a chicken if she will lay him an egg because he needs just one more, is taken on a barnyard tour in search of an animal that will fill his request.

DePalma, Mary Newell. *The Strange Egg*. Houghton Mifflin, 2001. A little bird tries to hatch a strange egg before a monkey tells her it is an orange.

Emmett, Jonathan. *Ruby in Her Own Time.* Illustrated by Rebecca Harry. Scholastic, 2004. Ruby is slower to develop than her siblings, until the day she flies further and higher than any of them.

Engelbreit, Mary. *Queen of Easter.* HarperCollins, 2006. Ann Estelle is not impressed with her new Easter hat until a robin lays eggs in it.

Fox, Mem. *Hunwick's Egg.* Illustrated by Pamela Lofts. Harcourt, 2005. When a storm sends a beautiful egg to Hunwick the bandicoot's burrow, he decides to give it a home and become its friend.

Graham, Bob. *Dimity Dumpty: The Story of Humpty's Little Sister.* Candlewick Press, 2007. What happened to Humpty Dumpty is legend. But how many know of his brave little sister?

Hills, Tad. *Duck & Goose.* Schwartz & Wade Books, 2006. Duck and Goose learn to work together to take care of a ball, which they think is an egg.

Jenkin-Pearce, Susie. *A Pal for Pugwug.* Illustrated by Tina Macnaughton. Gingham Dog Press, 2006. While waiting impatiently for his new brother or sister to hatch, Pugwug the penguin tries to play football with the egg.

Larsen, Kirsten. *Dora's Rainbow Egg Hunt.* Illustrated by Steven Savitsky.

Simon Spotlight/Nick Jr., 2006. Help Dora and Boots find colored eggs by peeking under movable flaps.

Maccarone, Grace. *Peter Rabbit's Happy Easter.* Illustrated by David McPhail. Scholastic, 2006. Inventing a new tradition, Peter Rabbit becomes the Easter Bunny.

McNamara, Margaret. *Eloise Breaks Some Eggs.* Illustrated by Tammie Speer-Lyon. Aladdin, 2005. Eloise's cooking lesson with Nanny and Cook is disastrous—or would be, if Eloise could not order room service. A Ready-to-Read book.

Sander, Sonia. *The Biggest Easter Egg.* Illustrated by the Artifact Group. Scholastic, 2006. Emily Elizabeth and Clifford the dog love decorating Easter eggs. But are there any eggs big enough for Clifford? An ostrich has the answer!

Schmauss, Judy Kentor. *Ted Saw an Egg.* Barron's, 2006. Ted finds a very large egg, from which an equally large chick hatches. Includes facts about eggs, a related activity, and word list. (A Beginning Reader.)

Waddell, Martin. *It's Quacking Time.* Illustrated by Jill Barton. Candlewick Press, 2005. A duckling and all his family happily await the hatching of his parents' new egg.

Poems

"Eggs" in *The Llama Who Had No Pajama: 100 Favorite Poems* by Mary Ann Hobermann. Illustrated by Betty Fraser. Harcourt, 2006.

"Humpty Dumpty" in *Mary Had a Little Jam and Other Silly Rhymes* by Bruce Lansky. Illustrated by Stephen Carpenter. Meadowbrook Press, 2004.

"Humpty Dumpty Sat on a Pot" in *Peter, Peter Pizza-Eater and Other Silly Rhymes* by Bruce Lansky. Illustrated by Stephen Carpenter. Meadowbrook Press, 2006.

"Humpty Dumpty" (Traditional)

Humpty Dumpty sat on a wall.

Humpty Dumpty had a great fall.

All the King's horses and all the King's men

Couldn't put Humpty together again.

Alphabet Activities

ABC Connect-the-Dots

Copy one pattern on page 60 for each child. Have the children connect the dots from A to Z to find the mystery picture.

ABC Humpty Dumpty

Enlarge and copy one each of the patterns on pages 61–62 for each child. Have the children color Humpty Dumpty and the brick wall. Humpty Dumpty then can be cut out and glued onto the appropriate spot on the wall page. Have the children point to each brick, saying the letter of the alphabet. Alternatively, individual bricks can be cut out and glued to the appropriate place on the wall.

Creative Activities

Toilet Paper Roll Egg Cup

Cut a 1" piece from a toilet paper roll for each child. Have the children decorate the roll with stickers or drawings. This size is perfect for holding an egg.

Easter Egg Hunt

Have the children participate in a good old-fashioned egg hunt. Be sure that all children get something.

Egg Matching Flannelboard

Cut a number of egg shapes from felt. Match the felt eggs into pairs. Decorate each pair in a unique style. Sort the pairs into two piles. Keep one pile, and pass out the others to the children. Place felt eggs up on the flannelboard, one at a time, and have the child with the matching egg place it beside them on the board.

Egg Shell Mosaic

Crush blown and dyed eggshells into small pieces. Have the children glue pieces together on a sheet of construction paper to form a mosaic.

Egg Tree

Have the children decorate purchased plastic eggs with crayons and stickers. Tie strings or ribbons onto the eggs and hang from a small branched tree.

Hatching Eggs

If facilities exist, eggs can be hatched in a classroom using an incubator. The process is totally fascinating for children to watch.

Creating Egg Characters

Make five eggs.

- Trace egg pattern onto white fun foam. For Easter eggs, use colored fun foam.
- Cut out all the pieces.
- If making Easter eggs, decorate eggs with ribbons or paint.
- Glue velcro to back.

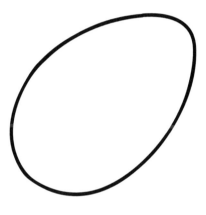

Egg

_gg

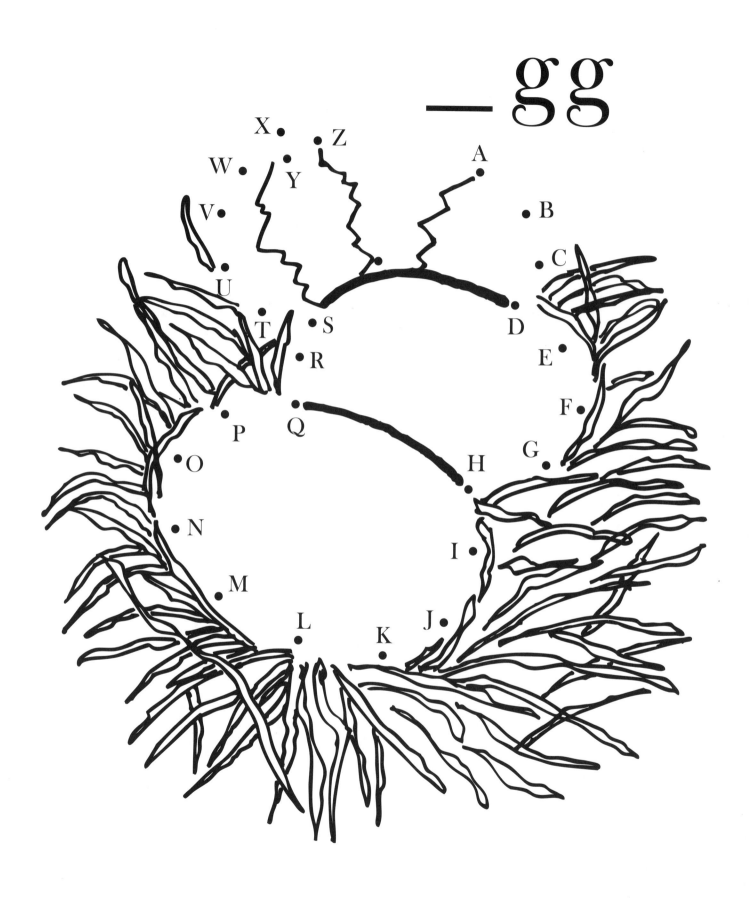

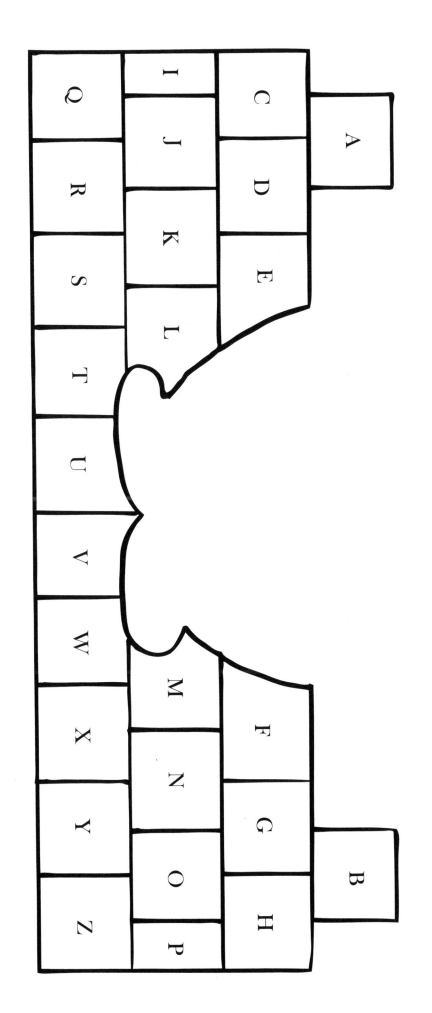

Humpty Dumpty Pattern

E E E E E E E E E E E

E   E

e e e e e e e e e e e e

e   e

Ee Ee Ee Ee Ee Ee

Ee   Ee

F — Fish

Introduction

You'll get a variety of responses when you introduce a fish theme. Some children will excitedly chatter about their aquariums, or their experiences fishing, while others will curl their noses at the thought of putting a worm on a hook! This topic would work well incorporated into a marine theme, as well as one of fishing as a sport. The "f" sound is one that can be practiced again and again.

Introductory Poem

It starts with "f" and ends with "ish." You'll find a gold one in a dish.

Finger Play Speller

- Use the finger play glove following the pattern and instructions on pages 13–16.
- Make one each of f, i, s, h for the glove using the patterns on pages 17–18.
- Make one fish finger play character using the pattern on page 68.

- Affix the fish finger play character in the center velcro tab of the glove.
- One by one, attach the f, i, s, h letters onto the glove. Pause between each one, focusing on the sounds and the blends: f fi fis fish. Once "fish" has been achieved, spell the word by pointing to the letters and saying them out loud.

Name Game

- Have the children think of the name of a person that begins with "f" (Freddy, Fernanda, Fern, etc.).
- Have children work on sentences that focus on the "f" sound (Freddy the fish flip-flops freely. Freda the fish fans her flowing fins. Etc.). Make the sentences as silly as possible.

Finger Plays

- Make five of the fish finger play character, using the pattern and instructions on page 68.
- Practice rhyming sounds with the finger plays. Use the ones provided,

or look for others. Use the finger play characters to count either up or down with the plays.

Count Down Rhyme

"Five Little Fish"

(Sung to the tune "Five Bran Muffins" on *Sidewalk Shuffle*. Sandra Beech. A&M Records, 1984.)

Five little fish in the farmer's pond,

Five little fish, swimming 'round and 'round.

A boy came fishing with his pole one day.

He caught a little fish, and he carried it away.

(Repeat for 4, 3, 2, 1)

No little fish in the farmer's pond,

No little fish, swimming 'round and 'round.

A boy came fishing with his pole one day.

Sorry little boy, no more fishing today.

Count Up Rhyme

"One Little Fish"

One little fish in the pond so blue,

Along came another, and then there were two.

Two little fish, heading out to sea,

Along came another, and then there were three.

Three little fish, swimming far from shore,

Along came another, and then there were four.

Four little fish—watch them splash and dive.

Along came another, and then there were five.

Resources for Storytime

Use some of these books and poems, or any of your favorites, to create a well-rounded storytime program.

Books

Berkes, Marianne Collins. *Over in the Ocean: In a Coral Reef.* Illustrated by Jeanette Canyon. Scholastic, 2005. Based on the traditional song "Over in the Meadow."

Boniface, William. *The Adventures of Max the Minnow.* Illustrated by Don Sullivan. Accord, 2000. A small fish sets out to become the biggest fish of all but learns to appreciate himself for who he is.

Cousins, Lucy. *Hooray for Fish!* Candlewick Press, 2005. Little Fish has all sorts of fishy friends in his underwater home, but loves one of them most of all.

Galloway, Ruth. *Figety Fish.* Tiger Tales, 2001. Sent out for a swim in the sea, Tiddler, a young fish who just can't keep still, sees many interesting creatures and one very dark cave.

Goldfinger, Jennifer P. *A Fish Named Spot*. Little, Brown and Company, 2001. When he feeds his pet fish dog biscuits, Simon's wish for a dog comes true in a most unusual way.

Lagonegro, Melissa. *Just Keep Swimming*. Random House, 2005.When Nemo worries that his too-small fin will keep him off the school swim team, his friend Dory encourages him. A "Step-Into-Reading" book.

LaReau, Kara. *Ugly Fish*. Illustrated by Scott Magoon. Harcourt, 2006. At first Ugly Fish likes being alone in his tank, but when he becomes lonely, he devises a better plan.

Lionni, Leo. *Fish is Fish*. Knopf Books for Young Readers, 2005. A fish and a tadpole learn of their differences.

Mills, Elizabeth. *Tick-Tock Sharks*. Illustrated by Delanna Bettoh. Scholastic, 2005. Rhyming text introduces telling time.

Pfister, Marcus. *Rainbow Fish Finds His Way*. North-South Books, 2006. When Rainbow Fish gets lost and separated from his family and friends during an undersea storm, he makes new friends that help him find his way home. See also *Rainbow Fish to the Rescue!* and *The Rainbow Fish*.

Rabe, Tish. *The Fish's Tale*. Illustrated by Jan Gerardi. Random House, 2003.

Sally and Conrad's pet fish describes the day spent with the Cat in the Hat.

Rohmann, Eric. *Clara and Asha*. Roaring Brook Press, 2005. Clara would rather play with her imaginary giant fish, Asha, than settle down to sleep.

Wood, Audrey. *Ten Little Fish*. Illustrated by Bruce Wood. Blue Sky Press, 2004. A simple underwater counting book.

Yoo, Tae-Eun. *The Little Red Fish*. Dial, 2007. A little boy explores a magical library with his friend, a little red fish.

Ziefert, Harriet. *Fish Wish*. Illustrated by Elliot Kreloff. Sterling Publishing, 2005. Part of the "I'm Going to Read" series.

Poems

"A Baby Sardine" by Spike Milligan in *The Usborne Book of Poems for Young Children* compiled by Philip Hawthorn. Illustrated by Cathy Shimmer. Usborne Books, 2004.

"A Catch," "Fish," and "Way Down Deep" from *The Llama Who Had No Pajama: 100 Favorite Poems* by Mary Ann Hoberman. Illustrated by Betty Fraser. Harcourt, 2006.

"The Fish" by Elizabeth Bishop in *A Family of Poems: My Favorite Poetry for Children* compiled by Caroline Kennedy. Illustrated by Jon J. Muth. Hyperion, 2005.

"The Fishes of Kempenfelt Bay" in *Alligator Pie* by Dennis Lee. Illustrated by Frank Newgeld. Key Porter Kids, 2001.

"Go A-Fishin'" in *See Saw Saskatchewan: More Playful Poems from Coast to Coast* by Robert Heidbreder. Illustrated by Scot Ritchie. Kids Can Press, 2003.

Alphabet Activities

ABC Connect-the-Dots

Copy one pattern on page 69 for each child. Have the children connect the dots from A to Z to find the mystery picture.

ABC Fish Pond

Enlarge and copy one each of the patterns on pages 70–71 for each child. Have the children color the pond and the fish and cut out the fish. The children can match the alphabet fish to the appropriate spot in the pond then glue them in place.

Creative Activities

Paper Plate Fish

Make a fish body for each child by gluing or stapling two paper plates together—convex sides out. Have the children draw eyes and mouths on their fish and make fins from scraps of paper.

Fish Pond

Have kids "go fishing" in the program room. Cut out some fish shapes from construction paper. Punch a hole near the mouth and attach a paper clip. Spread a number of fish in a small wading pool. Make fishing poles by using a piece of dowel with a string tied to it. At the end of the string, attach another paper clip. Open one prong of the paper clip to make a hook. Let each child catch a fish.

Fish Mobile

Children can create fish mobiles with five small fish cut from construction paper and two popsicle sticks. Glue popsicle sticks into an "X" formation. Tie pieces of string on each end of the sticks, and tie one at the center where the sticks meet. Attach fish to ends of string. Tie another piece of string above the mobile to hang it.

Aquarium Scene

Using a styrofoam meat tray, create an aquarium scene by gluing cutouts of weeds and fish onto the inside of the tray. Try National Geographic magazines for fish pictures.

Creating Fish Characters

Make five fish.

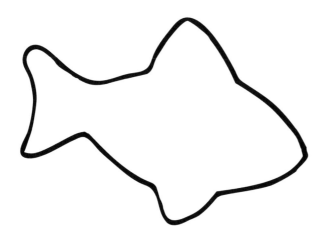

- Trace fish pattern onto grey fun foam.

- Cut out all the pieces.

- Apply fabric paint to create fins and tail.

- Glue on small roly eye.

- Glue velcro to back.

Fish

_ish

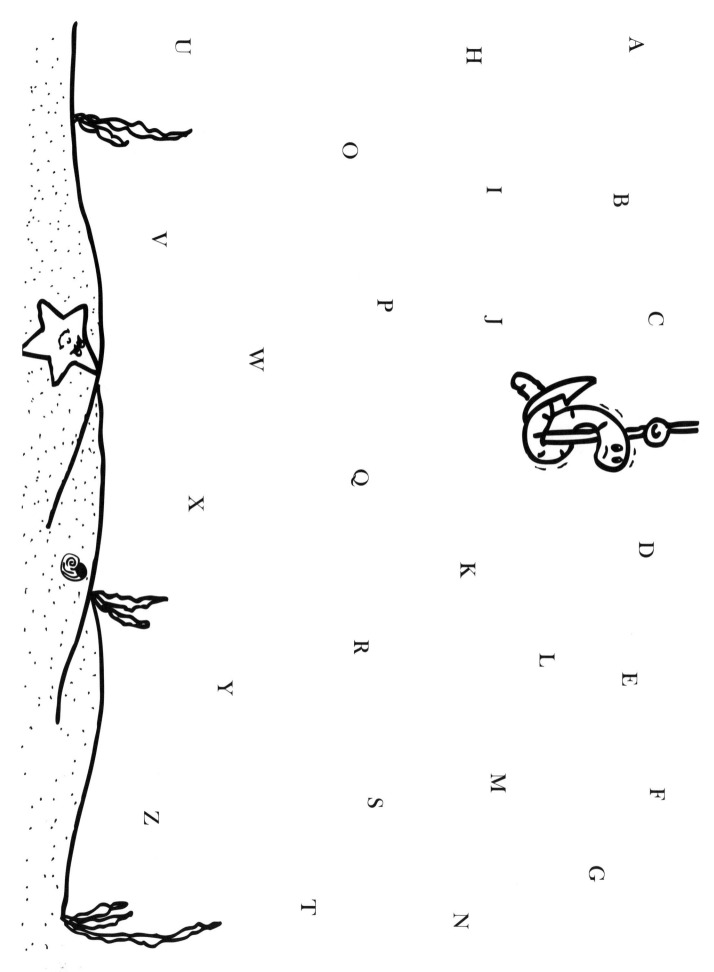

A

B

C

D

E

F

G

H

I

J

K

L

M

N

O

P

Q

R

S

T

U

V

W

X

Y

Z

Fish Patterns

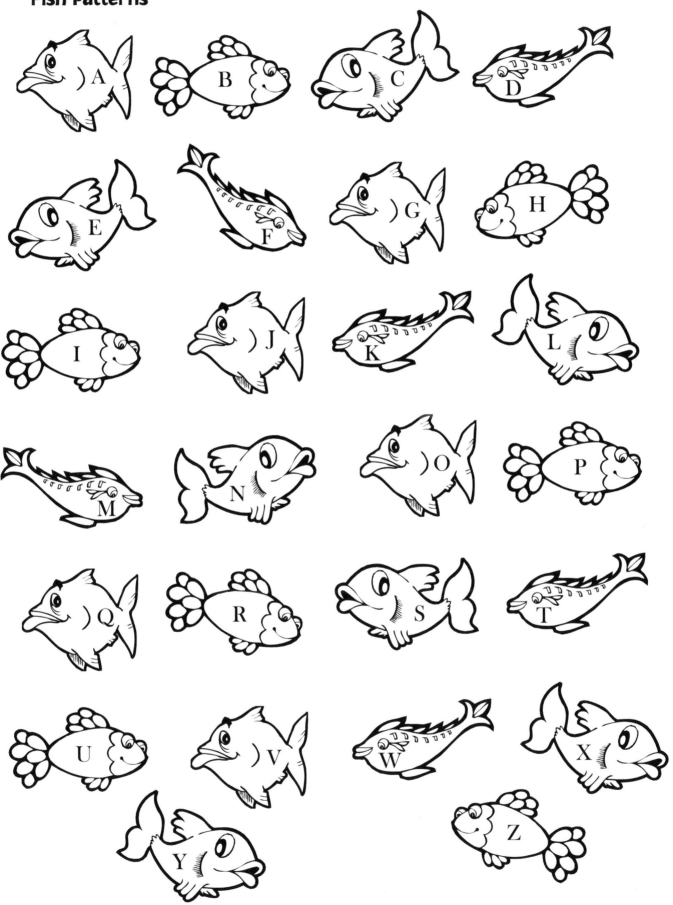

F F F F F F F F F F F F

F — F

f f f f f f f f f f f f

f — f

Ff Ff Ff Ff Ff Ff Ff Ff

Ff — — — — — — — — — — — — — — — — — — Ff

G — Ghost

Introduction

Children love to hear stories about ghosts and pretend to scare people by shouting "boo!" Try varying from "boo" to "oo" for a good vowel sound practice. The "g" sound might be practiced with a "grr" or two.

Introductory Poem

He starts with "g" and ends with "ost." A haunted house he likes the most.

Finger Play Speller

- Use the finger play glove following the pattern and instructions on pages 13–16.
- Make one each of g, h, o, s, t for the glove using the patterns on pages 17–18.
- Make one ghost finger play character using the pattern on page 77.
- Affix the ghost finger play character in the center velcro tab of the glove.
- One by one, attach the g, h, o, s, t letters onto the glove. Pause between

each one, focusing on the sounds and the blends: g gh gho ghos ghost. Once "ghost" has been achieved, spell the word by pointing to the letters and saying them out loud.

Name Game

- Have the children think of the name of a person that begins with "g" (Gordie, Graham, Gwen, etc.).
- Have children work on sentences that focus on the "g" sound (Gordie the ghost giggles and giggles. Gwen gets a good grip on a grim ghost. Etc.). Make the sentences as silly as possible.

Finger Plays

- Make five of the ghost finger play characters, using the pattern and instructions on page 77.
- Practice rhyming sounds with the finger plays. Use the ones provided, or look for others. Use the finger play characters to count either up or down with the plays.

Count Down Rhyme

"Five Frightened Ghosts"

Five frightened ghosts standing by the door.

The wind scared one,

OOOH, OOOH—

And then there were four.

Four frightened ghosts underneath a tree.

A branch scared one,

SNAP, SNAP—

And then there were three.

Three frightened ghosts look for evening dew.

The rain scared one,

PITTER, PATTER—

And then there were two.

Two frightened ghosts were not having fun.

A cat scared one,

MEOW, MEOW—

And then there was one.

One frightened ghost, standing on the lawn.

I scared him,

BOO, BOO—

And then he was gone.

Count Down Rhyme

"Five Little Ghosts"

(Sung to the tune "Five Bran Muffins" on *Sidewalk Shuffle*. Sandra Beech. A&M Records, 1984.)

Five little ghosts in a haunted house,

Five little ghosts, quiet as a mouse.

A witch came by with her cat one day.

She scared a little ghost, and it floated away.

(Repeat for 4, 3, 2, 1)

Resources for Storytime

Use some of these books and poems, or any of your favorites, to create a well-rounded storytime program.

Books

Amsden, Janet. *Grizzly Pete and the Ghosts*. Illustrated by John Beder. Firefly Books, 2002. A young ghost is assigned the task of scaring Grizzly Pete out of Paydirt.

Berenstain, Stan. *The Berenstain Bears Go on a Ghost Walk*. HarperFestival, 2005. Papa Bear is enthused about preparing for Bear Country School's Halloween Ghost Walk, but learns that "one person's fun is another person's nightmare."

Bianchi, John. *In a Dark, Dark House.* Penguin Putnam Young Readers, 2002. A familiar ghost story with a surprise ending.

Bright, Robert. *Georgie.* Scholastic, 2000. Georgie must find a new house to haunt.

Brunhoff, Laurent de. *Babar and the Ghost.* H. N. Abrams, 2001. The ghost of the Black Castle follows Babar and his family.

Calmenson, Stephanie. *The Teeny Tiny Teacher.* Illustrated by Denis Roche. Scholastic, 2002. A teeny tiny teacher takes her class for a walk and discovers a teeny tiny bone …

Cuyler, Margery. *Skeleton Hiccups.* Illustrated by S. D. Schindler. Margaret K. McElderry Books, 2002. A ghost tries to help a skeleton with hiccups.

De Groat, Diane. *Good Night, Sleep Tight, Don't Let the Bedbugs Bite.* SeaStar Books, 2002. Gilbert is excited about staying overnight at camp, until he hears about a ghost.

Herman, Gail. *The Big White Ghost.* Illustrated by Ken Edwards. Scholastic, 2003. When Clifford watches a scary movie, the screen falls on him, making him look like a ghost.

Klein, Abby. *Halloween Fraidy-Cat.* Illustrated by John McKinley. Blue Sky Press, 2006. Freddy is apprehensive about the haunted house that Chloe plans to have at her Halloween party but tries to hide his fear from his class-mates.

Kovalski, Maryann. *Omar's Halloween.* Fitzhenry & Whiteside, 2006. Omar dresses as a boring old ghost at Halloween. His Halloween is ruined—until the weather comes to his aid.

Krishnaswami, Uma. *The Closet Ghosts.* Illustrated by Shiraaz Bhabha. Children's Book Press, 2006. Anu finds a way to copy with a new school, a new home, and pesky ghosts in her closet.

O'Connell, Jennifer Barrett. *Ten Timid Ghosts.* Scholastic, 2000. A witch tries to scare ten ghosts out of a haunted house. See also *Ten Timid Ghosts on a Christmas Night.*

Vaughan, Marcia K. *We're Going on a Ghost Hunt.* Illustrated by Ann Schweninger. Silver Whistle, 2001. Trick-or-treaters imagine all sorts of spooky things on Halloween.

Winters, Kay. *The Teeny Tiny Ghost and the Monster.* Illustrated by Lynn Munsinger. HarperCollins, 2004. The teeny tiny ghost and his classmates enter a monster-making contest at school.

Poems

"Grim and Gloomy" by James Reeves in *The Usborne Book of Poems for Young Children* comp. by Philip Hawthorn. Illustrated by Cathy Shimmen. Usborne Books, 2004.

"Halloween Night" in *Seasons: A Book of Poems* by Charlotte Zolotow. Illustrated by Erik Blegvad. HarperTrophy, 2002.

Lewis, J. Patrick. *The House of Boo.* Illustrated by Katya Krenina. Simon & Schuster, 1998. A spooky read-aloud poem featuring three children dressed as ghosts.

"Whose Boo is Whose?" in *Exploding Gravy: Poems to Make You Laugh.* X. J. Kennedy. Illustrated by Joy Allen. Little, Brown and Company, 2002.

Alphabet Activities

ABC Connect-the-Dots

Copy one pattern on page 78 for each child. Have the children connect the dots from A to Z to find the mystery picture.

Haunted House Alphabet

Enlarge and copy one each of the patterns on pages 79–80 for each child. Have the children color the haunted house and the ghosts and cut out the ghosts. The children can match the alphabet ghosts to the appropriate spot on the haunted house picture then glue them in place.

Creative Activities

BOO-mask

Enlarge and copy one mask pattern from page 77 for each child. Have the children color and decorate the mask and then cut it out. Fold the tab and insert the Popsicle stick in it. Tape or glue the Popsicle stick in place.

Ghost Necklaces

Cut a small black circle from Bristol board. Glue on lima beans for ghosts, and add eyes with markers. Cut a hole in the top of the circle and add a string for a necklace.

Tissue Ghosts

This is an old favorite for a craft. Roll a Kleenex into a small ball. Place it in the center of another Kleenex. Wrap the Kleenex around the rolled Kleenex and tie with elastic. The ball becomes the head of the ghost. Draw on eyes and mouth with a marker.

Spooky Sounds

Play a tape of spooky Halloween sounds while doing one of the crafts.

Trick or Treat

You may choose to have the children dress up for the Halloween program. If they do, you may wish to give a little treat to each child when the program finishes.

Creating Ghost Characters

Make five ghosts.

- Trace ghost pattern onto white fun foam.

- Cut out all the pieces.

- Paint eyes and mouth using a black marker or black fabric paint.

- Optionally, you may wish to add a piece of an old necklace to look like chains.

- Glue velcro to back.

Ghost

BOO Mask Pattern

_host

Ghost Patterns

G G G G G G G G

G - - - - - - - - - - - - - - - - - - G

g g g g g g g g g g

g - - - - - - - - - - - - - - - - - - g

Gg Gg Gg Gg Gg

Gg - - - - - - - - - - - - - - - - Gg

H — Horse

Introduction

Pretend ponies are one of the most popular companions for young children. They delight in mounting a broomstick horse and galloping about the yard with it. Horse themes are suitable for any time of year, though I prefer an Autumn or Winter program, incorporated with other farm animals, or with sleigh rides. Encourage children to "neigh," as it again practices vowel sounds. The "h" sound can be practiced quietly in the program.

Introductory Poem

He starts with "h" and ends with "orse." He says "neigh, neigh" and gallops, of course.

Finger Play Speller

- Use the finger play glove following the pattern and instructions on pages 13–16.
- Make one each of h, o, r, s, e for the glove using the patterns on pages 17–18.

- Make one horse finger play character using the pattern on page 86.
- Affix the horse finger play character in the center velcro tab of the glove.
- One by one, attach the h, o, r, s, e letters onto the glove. Pause between each one, focusing on the sounds and the blends: h ho hor hors horse. Once "horse" has been achieved, spell the word by pointing to the letters and saying them out loud.

Name Game

- Have the children think of the name of a person that begins with "h" (Hans, Hannah, Hector, Henry, etc.).
- Have children work on sentences that focus on the "h" sound (Hans the horse has heavy hooves. Hannah hates sitting high on a hippo. Etc.). Make the sentences as silly as possible.

Finger Plays

- Make five of the horse finger play character, using the pattern and instructions on page 86.

- Practice rhyming sounds with the finger plays. Use the ones provided, or look for others. Use the finger play characters to count either up or down with the plays.

Count Down Rhyme

"Clip, Clip, Clop" (Sung to the tune "Three Blind Mice.")

Clip, clip, clop, clip, clip, clop
See the horses trot, see the horses trot
They trot all over the farmyard ground
They trot here and there and all around
One canters away with just one sound,
Clip, clip, clop.

(Repeat until all horses have been removed from glove.)

Count Down Rhyme

"Five Little Horses"

(Sung to the tune "Five Bran Muffins" on *Sidewalk Shuffle*. Sandra Beech. A&M Records, 1984.)

Five little horses in a field of hay,
Five little horses calling, "neigh, neigh, neigh."
A boy came by with a saddle one day,
He saddled up a horse and they galloped right away.
(Repeat for 4, 3, 2, 1)

Resources for Storytime

Use some of these books and poems, or any of your favorites, to create a well-rounded storytime program.

Books

Adams, Jean Ekman. *Clarence Returns to 831 Eggplant Avenue*. Illustrated by Jean Akman Adams. Rising Moon Press, 2003. Clarence the pig and Smoky the purple horse set out with some new friends to see the city. See also *Clarence Goes Out West and Meets a Purple Horse*.

Anderson, C. W. *Blaze and the Gray Spotted Pony*. Aladdin, 2001. Tommy and Billy spot a pony in a field, and Tommy wants it for his. One of many Blaze stories.

Bastedo, Jamie. *Free as the Wind: Saving the Horses of Sable Island*. Illustrated by Susan Tooke. Red Deer Press, 2006. Based on the true story of horses on Sable Island, Nova Scotia.

Bradley, Kimberly Brubaker. *The Perfect Pony*. Illustrated by Shelagh McNicholas. Dial, 2007. While searching for a fast pony to own, a young girl comes to realize that the "perfect" pony is not what she expected. One night when Starlight escapes, Haley's hard work pays off.

Cooper, Helen. *Sandmare*. Illustrated by Ted Dewan. Farrar, Straus and Giroux,

2003. Polly and her father draw a horse in the sand and she wishes her horse could be free.

Earhart, Kristin. *Patch*. Illustrated by Lisa Papp. Scholastic, 2006. Lauren is friendly with Sarah even after the new girl brags that her horse is much better than Lauren's, but when Sarah gets in trouble while riding in the woods, Lauren and her horse come to the rescue.

Earhart, Kristin. *Starlight*. Illustrated by Dan Andreasen. Scholastic, 2006. Haley has difficulty training her foal, Starlight, to come when she calls, and finally one night when Starlight escapes, Haley's hard work pays off.

Guest, Elissa Haden. *Iris and Walter and the Birthday Party*. Illustrated by Christine Davenier. Harcourt, 2006. At Walter's birthday party his guests are supposed to go for horseback rides, but his horse Rain has other plans on the day of the party.

Haas, Jessie. *Appaloosa Zebra: A Horse Lover's Alphabet*. Illustrated by Margot Apple. Greenwillow Books, 2002. A girl ponders the many different kinds of horses she will have when she gets older.

Hayden, Kate. *Horse Show*. DK Publishing, 2001. A reader about show riding and show ponies.

Hoffman, Alice. *Horsefly*. Illustrated by Steve Johnson and Lou Fancher. Hyperion, 2000. Jewel is afraid of everything until her grandfather gives her a special flying horse.

Koldofsky, Eleanor. *Clip-Clop*. Illustrated by David Parkins. Tundra Books, 2005. Young Consuela's day is marked by the horses she loves. There's the clip-clop-clink of the horse that pulls the milk wagon, the quick-trot clippety-clop of the beautiful brown tea wagon horse, and the lolop … lolop … lolop of the produce man's tired gray horse.

Puttock, Simon. *Horsey*. Illustrated by Russell Julian. Egmont, 2004. One night, when the baby is asleep, two stuffed toys, Horsey & Moomoo go on an adventure.

Sundberg, Peggy. *Lonesome the Little Horse: His Mountain Adventure*. Coyote Moon, 2002. Based on a true story, this book tells the adventure of a sad, mistreated horse who is different. Lonesome runs away, and learns a lesson the hard way. A happy ending.

Tazewell, Charles. *The Littlest Red Horse*. Illustrated by Frank Sofo. Ideals Publications, 2001. A merry-go-round horse attracts the attention of visitors with his seemingly magical abilities.

Ulmer, Michael. *H is for Horse: An Equestrian Alphabet*. Illustrated by

Gijsbert van Frankenhuyzen. Sleeping Bear Press, 2004. Ulmer introduces the fun and fundamentals of horses through an alphabet book.

Poems

"Dapple-Gray" in *Mary Had a Little Jam and Other Silly Rhymes* by Bruce Lansky. Illustrated by Stephen Carpenter. Meadowbrook Creations, 2004.

Hubbell, Patricia. *A Grass Green Gallop.* Atheneum, 1990. A collection of poems celebrating horses.

"Indigo Stallion" in *Bubblegum Delicious* by Dennis Lee. Illustrated by David McPhail. Toronto, ON: Key Porter, 2000.

"Johnny-Horse" in *MaMa Goose: Rhymes and Poems for the Little Ones* by Edelen Willie. Kansas City, MO: Andrews McMeel Publishing, 2003.

"Red Horse, White Horse, Black Horse, Gray" in *The Frogs Wore Red Suspenders.* Jack Prelutsky. Pictures by Petra Mathers. Greenwillow Books, 2002.

"Ride a Cock Horse" (traditional nursery rhyme)
Ride a cock horse to Banbury Cross
To see a fine lady upon a white horse
Rings on her fingers and bells on her toes
She shall have music wherever she goes

Alphabet Activities

ABC Connect-the-Dots

Copy one pattern on page 87 for each child. Have the children connect the dots from A to Z to find the mystery picture.

ABC Horse Puzzle

Enlarge and copy one pattern on pages 88–89 for each child. Glue the pages to Bristol board. Have the children color and cut out the pages. The puzzle can be assembled by following the alphabet.

Creative Activities

Horse in Farmyard

Enlarge and copy one horse pattern (below) for each child. Have the children color and cut out the horse, and glue it onto construction paper. Using Popsicle sticks, have the children make a fence for their horse.

Stick Pony

Create a two-dimensional horse's head from cardboard. Glue the head to a broomstick. Children can mount and ride the pony.

Giddy up Horse Box

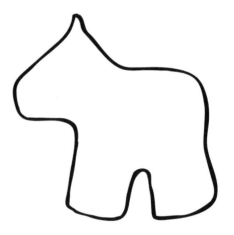

Find a television or computer monitor box or one of a similar size. Cut the top and bottom off. From the cut pieces, make a head and attach it to one side of the box. On the opposite side make a tail from the cut pieces. Attach a rope harness to the other two sides of the box. Let the children take turns riding the horse.

Spool Horse

Copy and cut out one head and one tail pattern (below) for each child. Have the children color their patterns. Glue head and tail onto a thread spool.

Galloping Classroom

Have the children make galloping sounds by patting their knees to a rhythm.

Creating Horse Characters

Make five horses.

- Trace horse pattern onto brown or other appropriate color of fun foam.
- Cut out all the pieces.
- Glue short pieces of yarn for tail and mane.
- Glue on medium-size roly eye.
- Glue velcro to back.

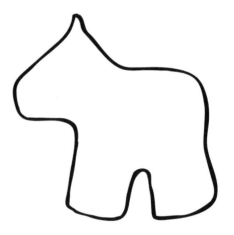

Horse

__ orse

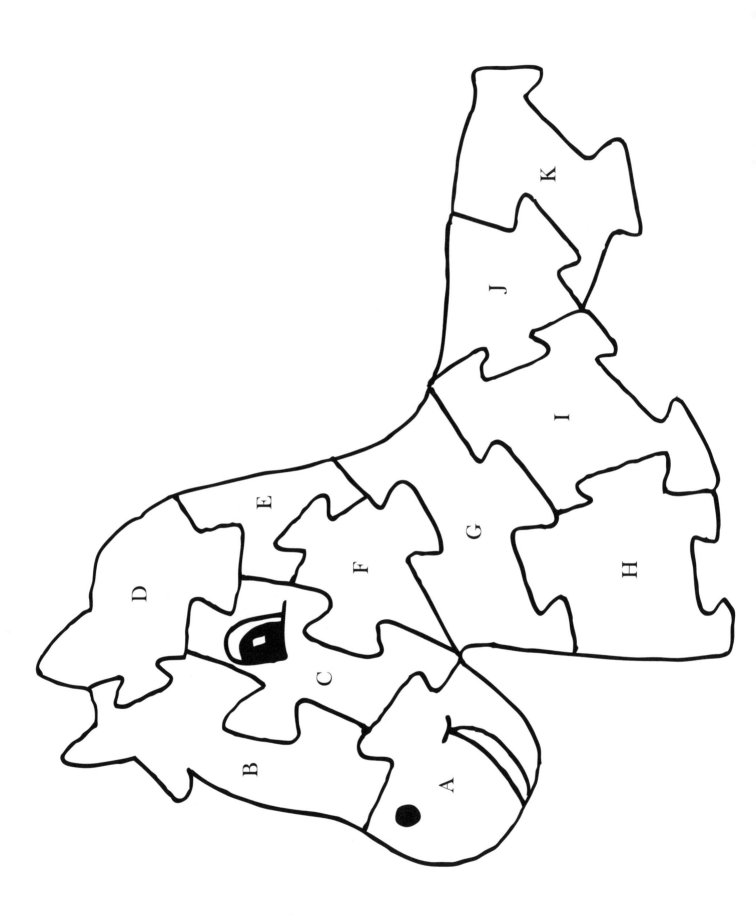

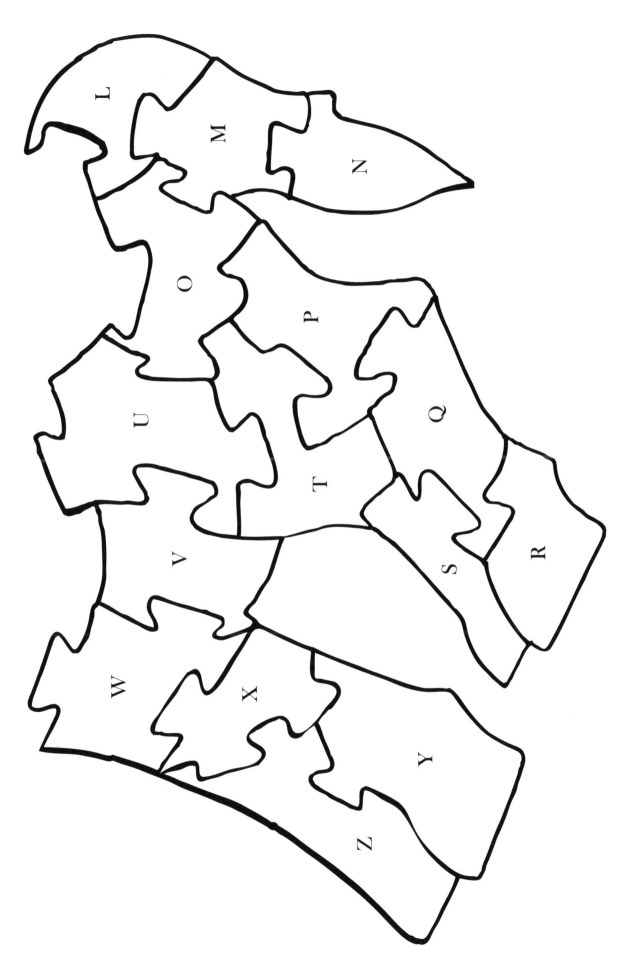

H H H H H H H H H H H H

H - - - - - - - - - - - - - - - - H

h h h h h h h h h h h h

h - - - - - - - - - - - - - - - - h

Hh Hh Hh Hh Hh Hh

Hh - - - - - - - - - - - - - Hh

I — Igloo

Introduction

Children, as well as adults, are fascinated with the construction of igloos. The short "i" sound is a necessary vowel sound to master. The long "i" sound can be practiced with words such as "ice".

Introductory Poem

It starts with "i" and ends with "gloo." With snow and ice we'll build one too.

Finger Play Speller

- Use the finger play glove following the pattern and instructions on pages 13–16.
- Make one each of i, g, l, o, o for the glove using the patterns on pages 17–18.
- Make one igloo finger play character using the pattern on page 94.
- Affix the igloo finger play character in the center velcro tab of the glove.
- One by one, attach the i, g, l, o, o letters onto the glove. Pause between each one, focusing on the sounds and the blends: i ig igl iglo igloo. Once "igloo" has been achieved, spell the word by pointing to the letters and saying them out loud.

Name Game

- Have the children think of the name of a person that begins with "i" (Ingrid, Izzie, etc.).
- Have children work on sentences that focus on the "i" sound (Ingrid is inside an igloo. Izzie isn't interested in iguanas. Etc.). Make the sentences as silly as possible.

Finger Plays

- Make five of the igloo finger play characters using the pattern and instructions on page 94.
- Practice rhyming sounds with the finger plays. Use the ones provided, or look for others. Use the finger play characters to count either up or down with the plays.

Count Up Rhyme

"Out on the Arctic"

(Sung to the tune "Down in the Valley.")

Out on the arctic, where the winds blow,
There were no igloos of ice and snow.
A weary traveler, wanted to stop.
He built an igloo, round on the top.

Repeat for 1, 2, 3, 4, 5

Count Up Rhyme

"One Little Igloo"

One little igloo, near the snow that blew.
A neighbor built another, and then there were two.

Two little igloos, round as round can be.
A neighbor built another, and then there were three.

Three little igloos heard the windy roar.
A neighbor built another, and then there were four.

Four little igloos keeping friends alive.
A neighbor built another, and then there were five.

Resources for Storytime

Use some of these books and poems, or any of your favorites, to create a well-rounded storytime program.

Books (Includes books on snow, Arctic, etc.).

Baker, Courtney. *Surprise! Snow Day!* Illustrated by Patti Goodnow. Scholastic, 2003. On a snowy day, a young girl enjoys making a snowman and building an igloo. A "Hello Reader" book.

Bania, Michael. *Kumak's Fish: A Tall Tale from the Far North*. Alaska Northwest Books, 2004. While fishing, Kumak hoods what seems like an enormous fish, and the entire village gets involved.

Bushey, Jeanne. *The Polar Bear's Gift*. Illustrated by Vladyana Krykorka. Red Deer Press, 2001. An Inuit legend.

George, Jean Craighead. *Arctic Son*. Illustrated by Wendell Minor. Hyperion, 1999. A baby boy is given an Inupiat name to go with his English one and grows up learning the traditional ways of the Arctic people.

George, Jean Craighead. *Nutik, the Wolf Pup*. Illustrated by Ted Rand. HarperCollins, 2001. When his older sister brings home two small wolf pups, Amaroq takes care of the one called Nutik.

Kusugak, Michael and Robert Munsch. *Arctic Stories.* Illustrated by Vladyana Krykorka. Annick Press, 1998. Inuit stories from Repulse Bay.

Kusugak, Michael. *My Arctic 1 2 3.* Illustrated by Vladyana Krykorka. Annick Press, 1996. A counting book featuring arctic themes.

Preszler, June. *Igloos.* Capstone Press, 2005. Includes mainly color illustrations.

Reynolds, Jan. *Frozen Land: Vanishing Cultures.* Lee & Low Books, 2007. Describes the traditional ways of the Inuit family. Good information for use in storytimes.

Sís, Peter. *A Small, Tall Tale from the Far, Far North.* Douglas & McIntyre, 2001. With the help of the Inuit, Jan Welzl survives a journey to the Arctic region in the 1800s. A book for older children, but interesting.

Steltzer, Ulli. *Building an Igloo.* Henry Holt & Company, 1995. Black and white photos are used to show how an Inuit father and son build an igloo out of snow.

Ulmer, Michael. *The Gift of the Inuksuk.* Illustrated by Melanie Rose. Sleeping Bear Press, 2004. A young girl builds stone men, called "inuksuk," to direct her father and brother home when they are lost in a storm.

Poems
"An Itty-Bitty Ibis"
An itty-bitty ibis built an igloo out of ice.
The itty-bitty ibis thought his igloo was quite nice.
An itty-bit of spring arrived—the rain began to fall.
And then it was the igloo that was itty-bitty small!

"This Is My Igloo"
This is my igloo of ice and of snow. (Make a dome shape with hands.)
These are the blocks that are placed row on row. (Place one fist on top of the other.)
This is the entrance— another small dome. (Make a small dome with one hand.)
Go through the entrance, and visit my home. (Walk fingers of the other hand into dome.)

Alphabet Activities
ABC Connect-the-Dots
Copy one pattern on page 95 for each child. Have the children connect the dots from A to Z to find the mystery picture.

Igloo Alphabet
Enlarge and copy one each of the patterns on pages 96–97 for each child.

Have the children color the mountains, sky, and igloo blocks and cut out the igloo blocks. The children can match the alphabet igloo blocks to the appropriate spot on the igloo picture then glue them in place.

Creative Activities

Egg Carton Igloos

Children can create a small village of igloos using egg cartons. Have the children cut out the igloos, decorate them, and glue them to a bristol board backing.

Ice Cube Drawings

Give each child an ice cube. Have them create pictures on the pavement or concrete. They can watch their pictures disappear.

Snowy Igloo Picture

Have each child draw an igloo or a winter scene on a piece of paper. Dampen each picture lightly with a sponge. While the picture is wet, shake salt over it. The salt will spread and crystallize to look like snowflakes.

Styrofoam Cup Igloo

Give each child one styrofoam cup and some miniature marshmallows. Children can cut down the size of the cup to resemble an igloo. Have the children glue marshmallows or cotton balls to the outside of the cup.

Sugar Cube Igloo

Give each child several sugar cubes and a small cup of a thick icing sugar and water mix. Have children construct their own igloo bases, or work together for a complete igloo.

Creating Igloo Characters

Make five igloos.

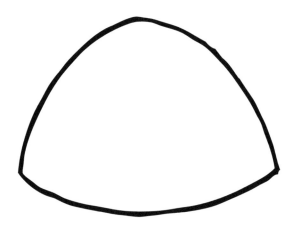

- Trace igloo pattern onto white fun foam.
- Cut out all the pieces.
- Apply block pattern and doorway with fabric paint.
- Glue velcro to back.

Igloo

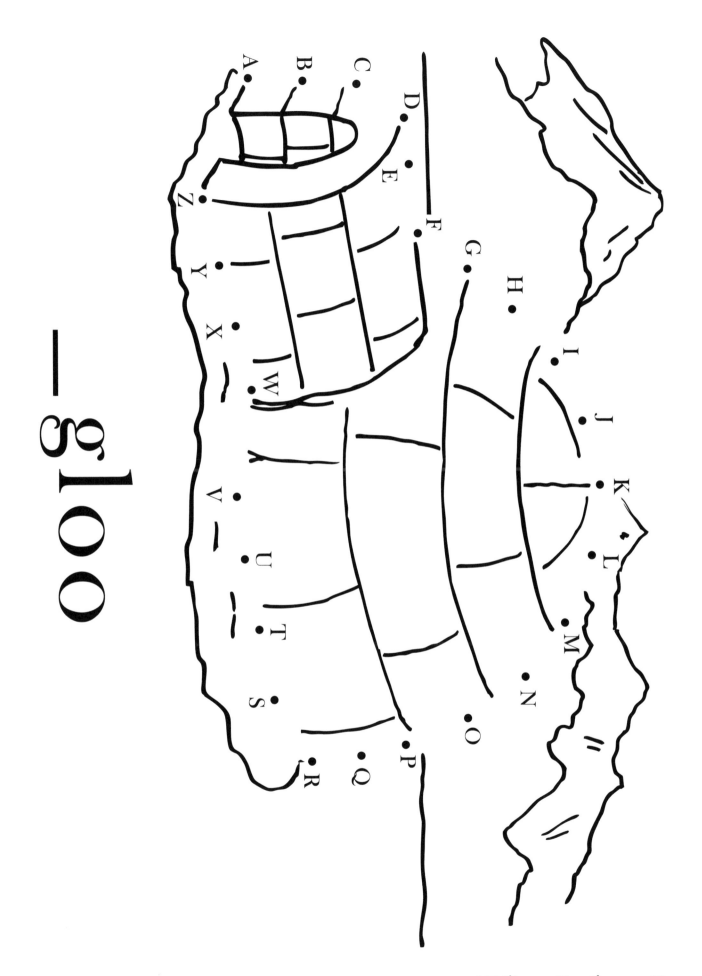

— gloo

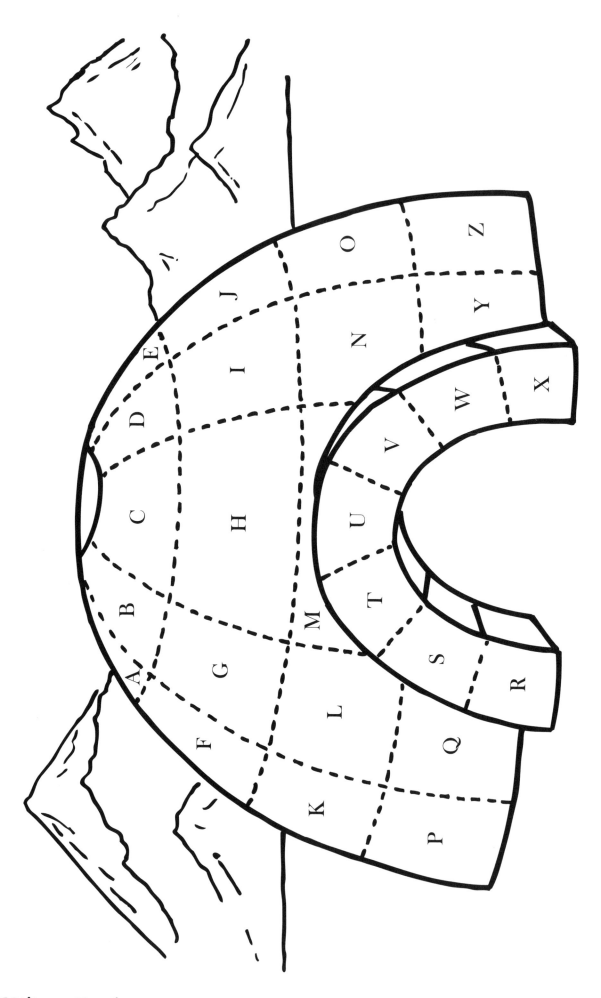

Igloo Blocks Pattern

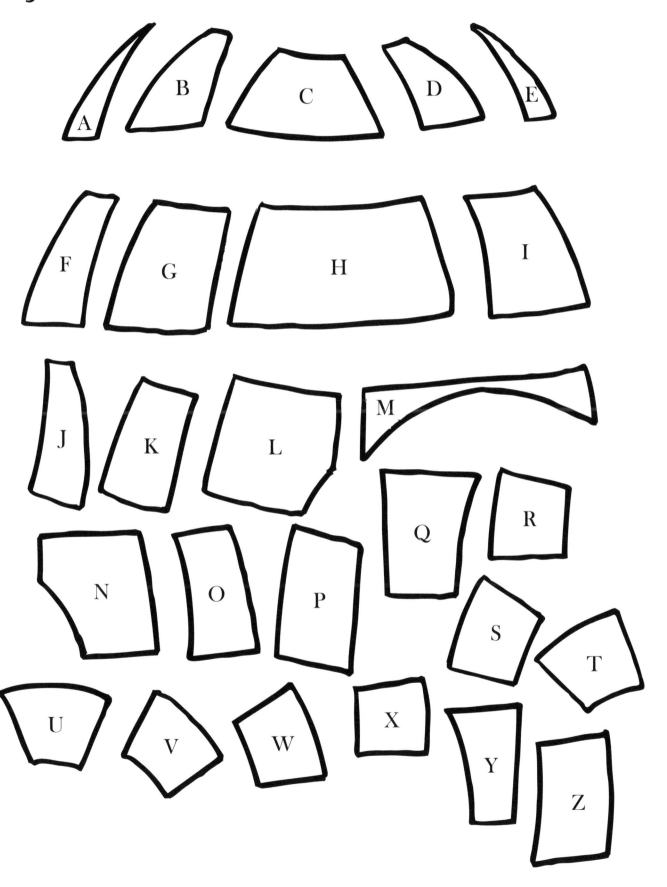

I I I I I I I I I I I I I I

I   I

i i i i i i i i i i i i i i i

i   i

Ii Ii Ii Ii Ii Ii Ii Ii

Ii   Ii

J – Jet

Introduction

Most any large transportation equipment will fascinate a child. Children love to pretend their toy jets are roaring across the sky. The "j" sound is not overly common, thus partnering the sound with a fascinating topic is desirable. The theme can be expanded to include airplanes of any type.

Introductory Poem

It starts with "j" and ends with "et."
At airports runways they might set.

Finger Play Speller

- Use the finger play glove following the pattern and instructions on pages 13–16.

- Make one each of j, e, t for the glove using the patterns on pages 17–18.

- Make one jet finger play character using the pattern on page 102.

- Affix the jet finger play character in the center velcro tab of the glove.

- One by one, attach the j, e, t letters onto the glove. Pause between each one, focusing on the sounds and the blends: j je jet. Once "jet" has been achieved, spell the word by pointing to the letters and saying them out loud.

Name Game

- Have the children think of the name of a person that begins with "j" (Jillian, Jeremy, John, etc.).

- Have children work on sentences that focus on the "j" sound (Jeremy joins the junior jet force. Jillian jokes about jelly juice. Etc.). Make the sentences as silly as possible.

Finger Plays

- Make five of the jet finger play character using the pattern and instructions on page 102.

- Practice rhyming sounds with the finger plays. Use the ones provided, or look for others. Use the finger play characters to count either up or down with the plays.

Count Down Rhyme

"Five Little Jets"

(Sung to the tune "Twinkle, Twinkle Little Star.")

Five little jets in the clear blue sky.

Five little jets, just watch them fly.

They fly left, they fly right,

One little jet flies out of sight.

How many jets are left to see?

Count them carefully with me.

Count Down Rhyme

"Five Jumbo Jets"

Five jumbo jets, by the hangar door.

One flew to Tokyo—that left four.

Four jumbo jets, shiny as can be.

One flew to Ireland—that left three.

Three jumbo jets in the sky of blue.

One flew to Canada—that left two.

Two jumbo jets in the morning sun.

One flew to Africa—that left one.

One jumbo jet—one and only one.

It flew to Germany—that left none!

Resources for Storytime

Use some of these books and poems, or any of your favorites, to create a well-rounded storytime program.

Books

Cefrey, Holly. *Super Jumbo Jets: Inside and Out.* Illustrated by Alessandro Bartolozzi, Leonello Calvetti, and Lorenzo Ceechi. Power Plus Books, 2002. Provides pictures and descriptions of jets.

Civardi, Anne. *Going on a Plane.* Illustrated by Stephen Cartwright. Usborne Books, 2005. A beginning reader that captures the experience of a plane ride.

Gutman, Anne. *Lisa's Airplane Trip.* Illustrated by Georg Hallensleben. Knopf, 2001. A toy takes a jumbo jet across the ocean, watches a movie, and gets a tour of the cockpit.

Hill, Lee Sullivan. *Jets.* Lerner Publishing Group, 2005. Introduces jet planes, how they work, and how they are used.

Jeffers, Oliver. *The Way Back Home.* Philomel Books, 2008. Stranded on the moon after his extraordinary airplane takes him into space, a boy meets a marooned Martian. The two work together to return to their homes.

McCarty, Peter. *Moon Plane.* Henry Holt & Company, 2006. A young boy looks at a plane in the sky and imagines flying one all the way to the moon.

Mitton, Tony, and Ant Parker. *Amazing Airplanes*. Kingfisher, 2005. Part of the "Amazing Machines" series.

Ormerod, Jan. *Miss Mouse Takes Off.* HarperCollins, 2001. A rag doll takes a trip to visit Granny.

Pallotta, Jerry. *The Jet Alphabet Book*. Illustrated by Rob Bolster. Charlesbridge, 2002. An introductory alphabet book with a jet theme.

Parks, Peggy J. *Fighter Pilot*. Kidhaven Press, 2006. Explores a career as a fighter pilot.

Pool, Steve. *I Wanna Be a Jet Pilot* (videorecording). Greg James Productions/ Marshmallow Marketing, 2000. Shows what it is like to fly a jet. Pay attention to public performance rights for videos in classroom use.

Spanyol, Jessica. *Go Bugs Go!* Candlewick Press, 2006. The adventures and misadventures of the Bugs as they travel in various types of automobiles, airplanes, and trains.

Stewart, Joel. *Me and My Mammoth*. MacMillan, 2005. Features various airplane models.

Sturges, Philemon. *I Love Planes!* Illustrated by Shari Halpern. HarperCollins, 2003. A child celebrates his love of planes by naming his favorite kinds and their notable characteristics.

Poems

"Stone Airplane" in *Falling Up* by Shel Silverstein. HarperCollins, 1996.

"Yankee Doodle Flew Through Space" in *Peter, Peter Pizza Eater and Other Silly Rhymes* by Bruce Lansky. Illustrated by Stephen Carpenter. Meadowbrook Press, 2006.

"Jellyfish Jetliner"
A jellyfish jumped on a flying jet,
Over to Juno it was hoping to get.
But the jet jerked and veered,
And the jellyfish jeered:
"I jolly-well won't get there yet!"

Alphabet Activities

ABC Connect-the-Dots

Copy one pattern on page 103 for each child. Have the children connect the dots from A to Z to find the mystery picture.

Airport Alphabet

Enlarge and copy one each of the patterns on pages 104–105 for each child. Have the children color the skyline and jets and cut out the jets. The children can match the alphabet jets to the appropriate spot on the airport picture then glue them in place.

Creative Activities

Airport Terminal

Turn the classroom or library into a pretend airport terminal. Demonstrate to the children the different parts of a trip, including buying the ticket, checking in the luggage, going through security, and finally boarding the plane.

Paper Jets

Have the children design their own paper jet patterns, or follow simple patterns from a book. Have the children pretend they are at an airport while launching their jets.

Pilot Visitor

If living in a city, it might be possible to arrange a visit from a pilot or a flight attendant. Children will be eager to hear what it is like working on an airplane.

String Art Jet

Have each child draw an outline of a jet on a piece of cardboard. Have them glue heavy string to the outline of the jet. Give each child a piece of tin foil and have them cover the picture. As the children press and shape the foil around the covered string, the shape of the jet will appear.

Creating Jet Characters

Make five jets.

- Trace jet pattern onto grey fun foam.
- Cut out all the pieces.
- Apply windows and features with black fabric paint.
- Glue velcro to back.

Jet

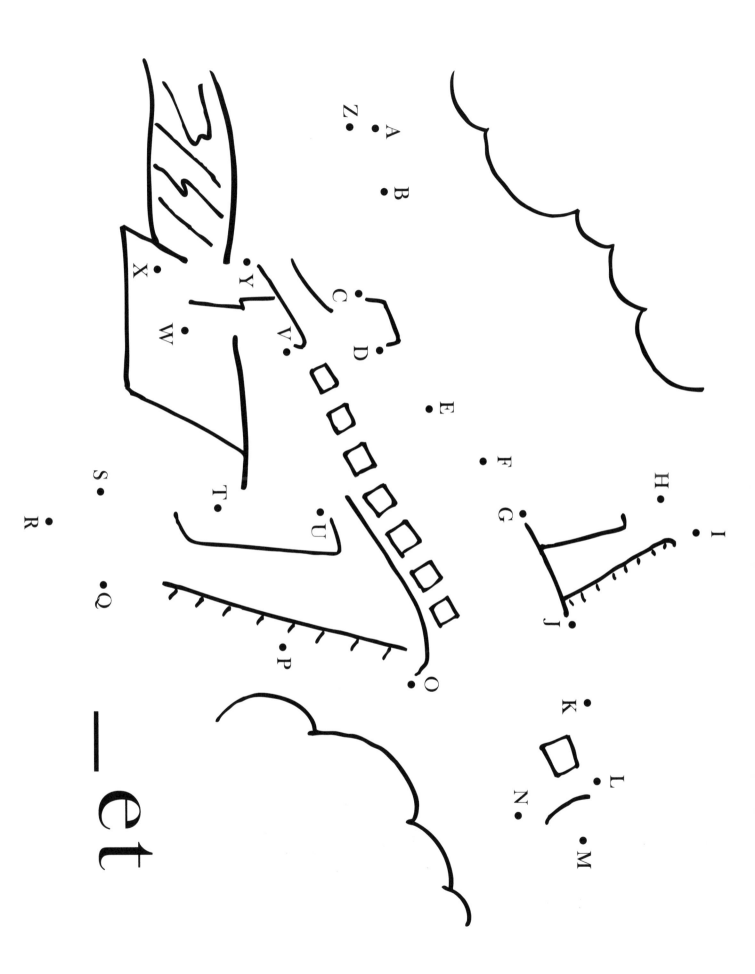

_et

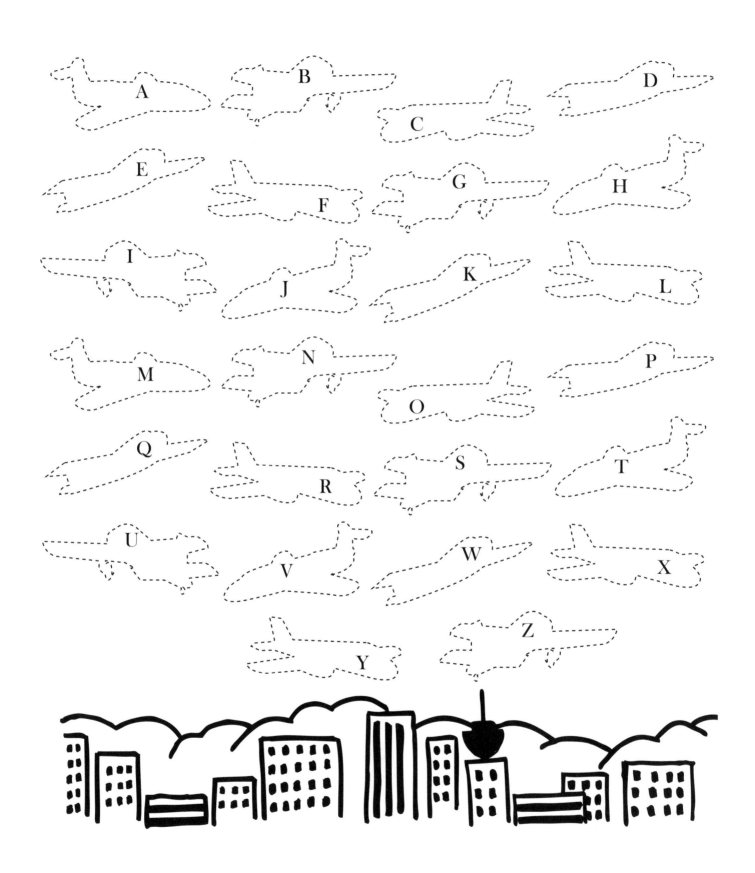

Jet Patterns

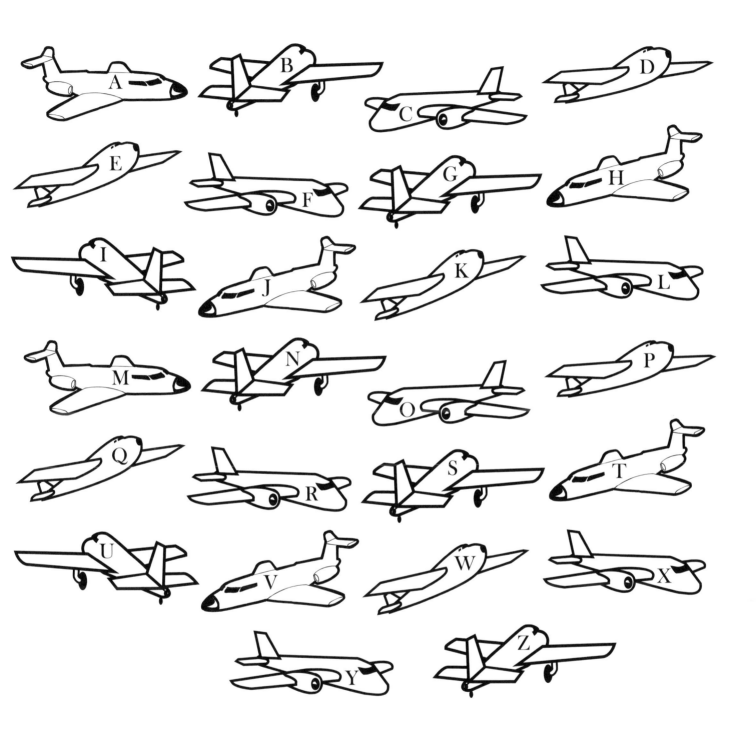

J J J J J J J J J J J J J

J   J

j j j j j j j j j j j j j j j

j   j

Jj Jj Jj Jj Jj Jj Jj Jj

Jj   Jj

K – Kite

Introduction

Despite all the modern toys and gadgets, flying a homemade kite is as much of a thrill for children as it was decades ago. The hard "k" sound requires practice.

Introductory Poem

It starts with "k" and ends with "ite"

With strings they fly to a great height.

Finger Play Speller

- Use the finger play glove following the pattern and instructions on pages 13–16.

- Make one each of k, i, t, e for the glove using the patterns on pages 17–18.

- Make one kite finger play character, using the pattern on page 110.

- Affix the kite finger play character in the center velcro tab of the glove.

- One by one, attach the k, i, t, e letters onto the glove. Pause between each one, focusing on the sounds

and the blends: k ki kit kite. Once "kite" has been achieved, spell the word by pointing to the letters and saying them out loud.

Name Game

- Have the children think of the name of a person that begins with "k" (Kevin, Kaiden, Kelly, etc.).

- Have children work on sentences that focus on the "k" sound (Kelly kicks a kite to Kenya. Kaiden has a kind kangaroo. Etc.). Make the sentences as silly as possible.

Finger Plays

- Make five of the kite finger play character using the pattern and instructions on page 110.

- Practice rhyming sounds with the finger plays. Use the ones provided, or look for others. Use the finger play characters to count either up or down with the plays.

Count Down Rhyme

"In the Sky" (Sung to the tune "Sur le pont d'Avignon.")

In the sky, way up high,

Five wee kites fly, five wee kites fly.

One swirls up, one swirls down.

One wee kite lands on the ground.

Count Up Rhyme

"One Little Kite"

One little kite in the sky so blue.

Johnny flew another one, and that made two.

Two little kites soaring near a tree.

Suzie flew another one, and that made three.

Three little kites, watch how high they soar.

Pedro flew another one, and that made four.

Four little kites, see them climb and dive.

Maku flew another one, and that made five.

(As an alternative to pre-selected names, substitute names of children in program.)

Resources for Storytime

Use some of these books and poems, or any of your favorites, to create a well-rounded storytime program.

Books

Baumgart, Klaus. *Laura's Secret*. Wilton, TigerTales, 2004. When Tommy is teased because his homemade kite does not fly well, his older sister, Laura, asks her secret star for help.

Berenstain, Stan & Jan. *We Like Kites*. Random House, 2004. While flying kites one summer day, Sister and Brother Bear encounter many other kinds of kites.

Demi, Hitz. *Kites: Magic Wishes That Fly Up to the Sky*. Dragonfly Books, 2000. A gorgeous story about the history, traditions, and legends surrounding kites.

Foreman, Mike. *Cat and Canary*. Random House, 2003. Cat wishes he could fly like Canary, and when he finds a kite, it is too much of a temptation.

Hall, Bruce. *Henry and the Kite Dragon*. Illustrated by William Low. Philomel Books, 2004. Based on true events, two rival groups of children representing two different cultures come face to face, and when they do, they find they share much more than just the same sky.

Lies, Brian. *Hamlet and the Enormous Chinese Dragon Kite*. Houghton Mifflin, 2003. Hamlet buys a big beautiful kite that lifts him off his feet for an aerial adventure.

Lin, Grace. *Kite Flying*. Knopf, 2002. It's a good day for kites, and the whole family makes a trip to the craft store for supplies to make and fly a kite.

Mayer, Mercer. *Shibumi and the Kitemaker*. Marshall Cavendish, 1999. After seeing the disparity between the conditions of her father's palace and the city beyond its walls, the Emperor's daughter has the royal kitemaker build a huge kite to take her away from it all.

Pilegard, Virginia. *Warlord's Kites*. Illustrated by Nicolas Debon. Pelican Publishing, 2004. When the warlord's palace is attacked, Chuan and his friend, Jing Jing, find an ingenious way to scare them off using simple kites.

Reddix, Valerie. *Dragon Kite of the Autumn Moon*. Illustrated by Jean & Mou-Sien Tseng. William Morrow & Co., 1992. When grandfather is sick, Tad-Tin goes out to fly his special dragon kite so that it can take all their troubles away with it.

Rey, Margaret. *Curious George Flies a Kite*. Illustrated by H. A. Rey. Boston, MA: Houghton Mifflin, 1999. Curious George's kite flying becomes a fun-filled adventure.

Torres, Leyla. *Kite Festival*. Farrar, Straus and Giroux, 2004. A family stumbles upon a kite festival and, with quick thinking and ingenuity, they put together an entry.

Wright, Sue. *The Kite*. Scholastic, 2005. Adapted from the original episode of "Davey and Goliath."

Yolen, Jane. *The Emperor and the Kite*. Puffin, 2002. When the emperor is imprisoned in a distant tower, it is his tiniest daughter who saves him with her kite.

Poems

"Kite" (anon.) in *The Usborne Book of Poems for Young Children* compiled by Philip Hawthorn. Illustrated by Cathy Shimmer. Usborne Books, 2004.

"The Wind" in *A Child's Garden of Verses* by Robert Louis Stevenson. Illustrated by Tasha Tudor. Simon & Schuster, 1999.

"I Wish I Was a Little Kite"

I wish I was a little kite,
A-flying in the sky.
I'd dip and swirl a 'way down low,
And then I'd fly up high.

Alphabet Activities

ABC Connect-the-Dots

Copy one pattern on page 111 for each child. Have the children connect the dots from A to Z to find the mystery picture.

Kite Bow Alphabet

Enlarge and copy one each of the patterns on pages 112–113 for each child. Have the children color the kite and the bows, and cut out the bows. The children can then match the alphabet bows to the appropriate spot on the kite tail then glue them in place.

Creative Activities

Make a Simple Kite

Have children design their own kite pattern, or take a piece of construction paper and cut it into a diamond shape. Cut ribbon for a kite tail and attach one to each kite. Have the children add shapes to the tail and then decorate their kites. Have a flying contest outdoors.

Dragon Kite

To create a dragon kite, first cut out a kite in the shape of a dragon's head, one for each child. Have the children cut out dragon scales, a mouth, and teeth. They can attach paper cups or egg carton pieces to make eyes for the dragon and can add colorful crepe paper streamers to the end of the kite.

Kite Name Tags

Make a kite shape for each child. Have the children color and cut out the kite. Write the name of the child on his or her kite with help from the child. Attach string for a tail and the neck piece.

Kite Shapes

Show a variety of different kites. Have the children discuss the shapes and draw the different shapes on a piece of paper.

Creating Kite Characters

Make five kites.

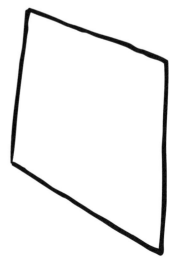

- Trace kite pattern onto any color of fun foam.
- Cut out all the pieces.
- Attach a small piece of string for kite tail.
- Tie small bows to the tail with ribbon.
- Optionally, apply a pattern to the kite with fabric paint.
- Glue velcro to back.

Kite

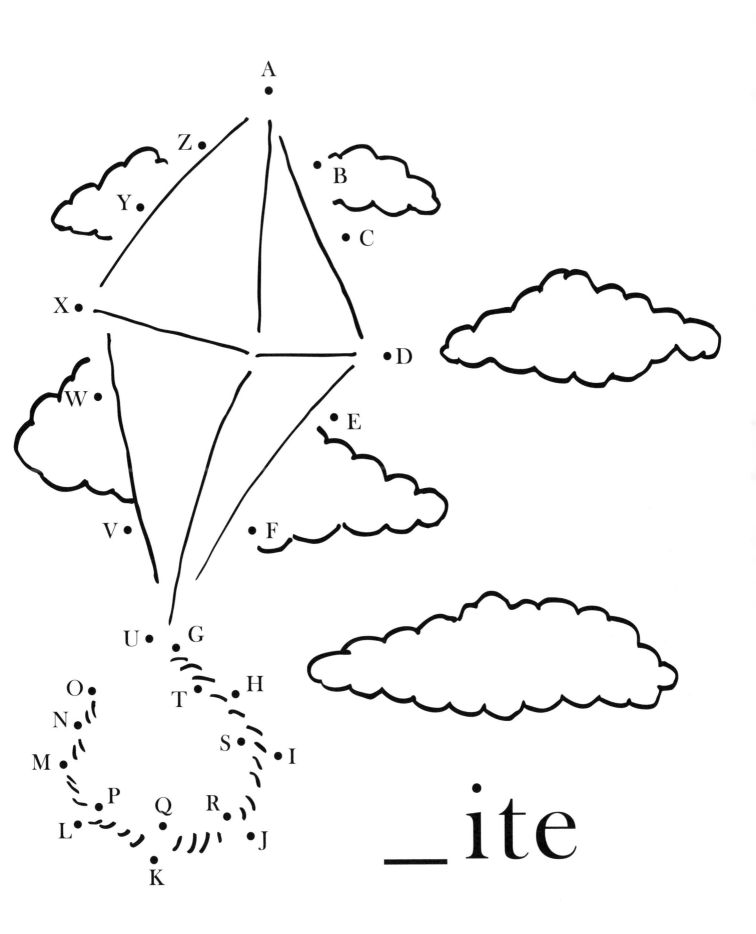

_ite

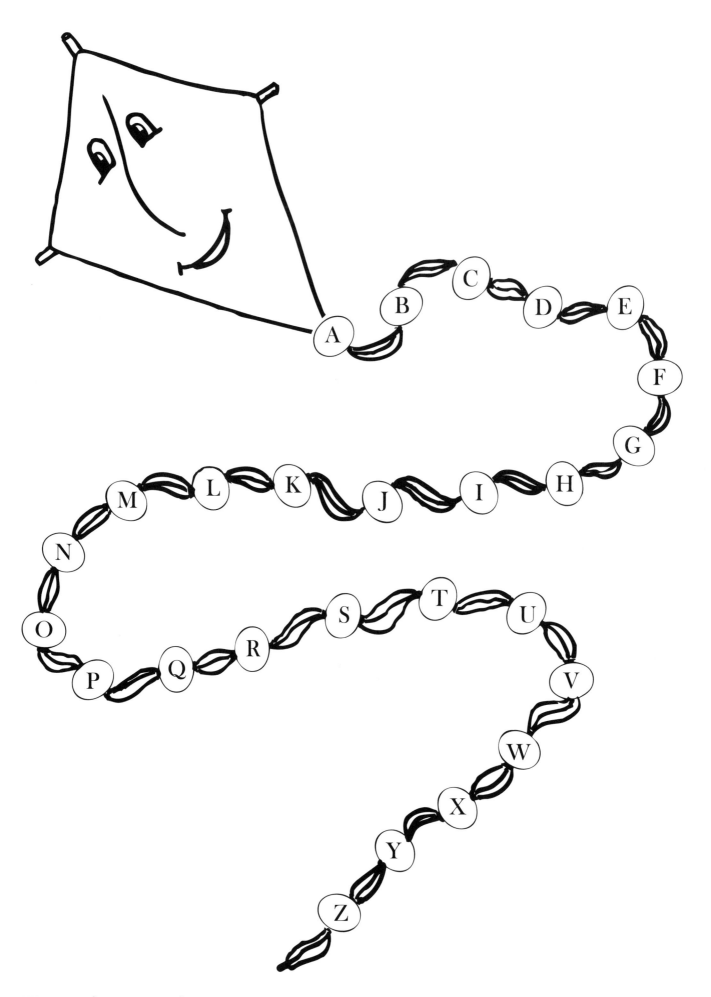

Bow Patterns

K K K K K K K K K K K K

K K

k k k k k k k k k k k k

k k

Kk Kk Kk Kk Kk Kk

Kk Kk

L — Lion

Introduction

What child can resist pretending to be a fierce, roaring lion? Naturally you'll need time to get the roars out of the room. After that, pretend that the lion is growling a quiet "lllll" sound.

Introductory Poem

He starts with "li" and ends with "on."
He likes to roar—for him it's fun.

Finger Play Speller

- Use the finger play glove following the pattern and instructions on pages 13–16.

- Make one each of l, i, o, n for the glove using the patterns on pages 17–18.

- Make one lion finger play character using the pattern on page 118.

- Affix the lion finger play character in the center velcro tab of the glove.

- One by one, attach the l, i, o, n letters onto the glove. Pause between each one, focusing on the sounds and the blends: l li lio lion. Once "lion" has been achieved, spell the word by pointing to the letters and saying them out loud.

Name Game

- Have the children think of the name of a person that begins with "l" (Leo, Lenny, Laura, etc.).

- Have children work on sentences that focus on the "l" sound (Laura likes laughing with a large lion. Lenny the lion loves little lollipops. Etc.). Make the sentences as silly as possible.

Finger Plays

- Make five of the lion finger play characters using the pattern and instructions on page 118.

- Practice rhyming sounds with the finger plays. Use the ones provided, or look for others. Use the finger play characters to count either up or down with the plays.

Count Up Rhyme

"One Fierce Lion" (Sung to the tune "Frère Jacques.")

One fierce lion, one fierce lion—
Hear him roar, hear him roar?
Calling for another, calling for another.
There's one more, there's one more.

Repeat for 2, 3, 4

Count Up Rhyme

"One Little Lion"

One little lion, roaring at the zoo.
Called for another: ROAR!
Then there were two.

Two little lions, underneath a tree.
Called for another: ROAR, ROAR!
Then there were three.

Three little lions who heard a distant roar.
Called for another: ROAR, ROAR, ROAR!
Then there were four.

Four little lions, happy and alive.
Called for another: ROAR, ROAR, ROAR, ROAR!
Then there were five.

Resources for Storytime

Use some of these books and poems, or any of your favorites, to create a well-rounded storytime program.

Books

Abercrombie, Barbara. *The Show-and-tell Lion*. Illustrated by Lynne Avril Cravath. Margaret K. McElderry Books, 2006. When Matthew has nothing for show-and-tell, he brags about haaving a lion living at the house.

Axtell, David. *We're Going on a Lion Hunt*. MacMillan Children's Books, 2000. Two girls set out bravely in search of a lion through long grass, a swamp, and a cave.

Conover, Chris. *The Lion's Share*. Farrar, Straus and Giroux, 2003. With the help of two animal fishermen, a young winged lion learns to read, to love books, and to fly properly.

Edwards, Pamela. *Roar: A Noisy Counting Book*. Illustrated by Henry Cole. HarperCollins, 2000. A lion cub's roar frightens away other colorful animals that he wants to play with—until he encounters nine other lion cubs.

Fatio, Louise. *The Happy Lion*. Knopf, 2004. When his cage door is accidentally left open, a friendly lion in a small zoo decides to visit all the people who have visited him.

Horácek, Petr. *Silly Suzy Goose.* Candlewick Press, 2006. Suzy longs to be different from all the other geese, but learns that imitating a lion may not be the best way to express her individuality.

Jensen, Patricia. *Gentle Little Lion.* Illustrated by Marcelle Geneste. Reader's Digest Young Families, 2001. By roaring for the first time, little lion lets his father know he can stop worrying about his not acting like a lion.

Kasza, Keiko. *The Mightiest.* Putnam, 2001. The lion, the bear, and the elephant compete to see who can do the best job in scaring a tiny old woman, but she has a surprise for them.

Knudsen, Michelle. *Library Lion.* Illustrated by Kevin Hawkes. Candlewick Press, 2006. A lion starts visiting the local library but runs into trouble as he tries to both obey the rules and help his librarian friend.

Lang, Audrey. *Baby Lion.* Fitzhenry & Whiteside, 2004. A baby lion discovers a world that is both exciting and dangerous, but it is through play that the lion learns the most valuable lesson.

Scheffler, Ursel. *Be Brave, Little Lion!* North-South Books, 2001. When Lea the lion cub sets off exploring on her own, she learns about the difference between cowardice and caution.

Yaccarino, Dan. *Deep in the Jungle.* Atheneum, 2000. After being tricked into joining the circus, an arrogant lion escapes and returns to the jungle where he lives peacefully with the animals he used to terrorize.

Poems

"The Lion" by Ogden Nash in *The Usborne Book of Poems for Young Children* compiled by Philip Hawthorn. Illustrated by Cathy Shimmen. Usborne Books, 2004.

"A Pride of Broccolions" in *Scranimals* by Jack Prelutsky. Illustrated by Peter Sís. Greenwillow Books, 2002.

"A Lazy Lion"

A lazy lion lay on the plain,

While lazily licking his lion's mane.

He licked and he licked with his long lion tongue,

Then the lion lamented, "Alas, I'm all done!"

Alphabet Activities

ABC Connect-the-Dots

Copy one pattern on page 119 for each child. Have the children connect the dots from A to Z to find the mystery picture.

A–Z Letter Lions

Enlarge and copy 26 of the lion patterns and one set of the alphabet on page 120 for each child. Have the children color the lions and cut them out. The children can either cut and paste the letters of the alphabet on the lions, or write the letters themselves. Using a hole-punch, make four holes in each of the lions (A and Z need only two holes). Tie each letter lion to the next lion with pieces of string or yarn.

Creative Activities

Fiercest Lion Contest

One by one, have the children imitate a lion. Have prizes for the fiercest, loudest, cutest, etc.

Lion Mask

Have children draw and color lion features onto a paper plate. Allow children to further decorate their lions with whiskers, ears, and a larger mane. Cut out holes for eyes. Punch one hole on each side of the plate and attach a piece of string to each hole.

Paper Lion

Copy one pattern from page 121 for each child onto construction paper. Have children color and cut out pieces. Fold lion's body on dotted line. Glue head to front and tail to back.

Wild Cats

Look for pictures of lions, tigers, cheetahs, panthers, etc., in wildlife magazines or on the Internet. Show the pictures and discuss with the children the differences and similarities with these animals.

Creating Lion Characters

Make five lions.

- Trace lion and head patterns onto brown fun foam.
- Trace mane pattern onto yellow or gold fun foam.
- Cut out all the pieces.
- Glue one mane to each lion.
- Glue one head to each mane.
- Attach small roly eyes.
- Apply mouth and features with black fabric paint.
- Glue velcro to back.

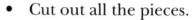

Mane

Head

Lion

___ ion

A-Z Letter Lion Pattern

A B C D E F G
H I J K L M N
O P Q R S T U
V W X Y Z

Paper Lion Pattern

L L L L L L L L L L L L L L L

L — — — — — — — — — — — — — — — — L

l l l l l l l l l l l l l l l l l

l — — — — — — — — — — — — — — — — l

Ll — Ll — Ll — Ll — Ll — Ll — Ll

Ll — — — — — — — — — — — — — — — Ll

M — Mouse

Introduction

Children often think of mice as cute little pets, although their parents might strongly disagree. A theme of mice is suitable to present at any time of the year, with no leaning to any particular season. The "squeak, squeak" sound emphasizes a long "e," while the "m" sound can be quietly practiced during parts of the program.

Introductory Poem

She starts with "m" and ends with "ouse."

One might scamper in your house.

Finger Play Speller

- Use the finger play glove following the pattern and instructions on pages 13–16.
- Make one each of m, o, u, s, e for the glove using the patterns on pages 17–18.
- Make one mouse finger play character using the pattern on page 128.

- Affix the mouse finger play character in the center velcro tab of the glove.
- One by one, attach the m, o, u, s, e letters onto the glove. Pause between each one, focusing on the sounds and the blends: m mo mou mous mouse. Once "mouse" has been achieved, spell the word by pointing to the letters and saying them out loud.

Name Game

- Have the children think of the name of a person that begins with "m" (Marvin, Maya, Mary, etc.).
- Have children work on sentences that focus on the "m" sound (Mary is marvelous at making moose muffins. Marvin the mouse munches on mangoes. Etc.). Make the sentences as silly as possible.

Finger Plays

- Make five of the mouse finger play characters using the pattern and instructions on page 128.

- Practice rhyming sounds with the finger plays. Use the ones provided, or look for others. Use the finger play characters to count either up or down with the plays.

Count Down Rhyme

"Five Little Mice" (Adapted)
(Sung to the tune "One Elephant" by Sharon, Lois, and Bram.)
Five little mice went out one day
Looking for food along the way.
Along came kitty-cat, sleek and black ...
And only four little mice came back.

(Repeat for 4, 3, 2, 1)

Count Up Rhyme

"One Little Mouse"
One little mouse, with a nibble and a chew
Called for a friend ... SQUEAK!
And then there were two.

Two little mice, quick as quick can be
Called for a friend ... SQUEAK, SQUEAK!
And then there were three.

Three little mice as they scampered 'round the floor
Called for a friend ... SQUEAK, SQUEAK, SQUEAK!

And then there were four.
Four little mice, with another to arrive
Called for a friend ... SQUEAK, SQUEAK, SQUEAK, SQUEAK!
And then there were five.

Resources for Storytime

Use some of these books and poems, or any of your favorites, to create a well-rounded storytime program.

Books

Asch, Frank. *Mrs. Marlowe's Mice.* Illustrated by Devin Asch. Kids Can Press, 2007. Suspected of being a mouse sympathizer, Mrs. Marlowe must use style and wit to save her mice from certain doom.

Ada, Alma Flor. *Friend Frog.* Illustrated by Lori Lohstoeter. Scholastic, 2000. Field mouse wonders if he can be friends with a frog who is so different from him.

Benjamin, A. H. *Little Mouse and the Big Red Apple.* Scholastic, 2000. A mouse, struggling to carry a big apple, does not want to share with the animals who help along the way. See also *Mouse, Mole and the Falling Star.*

Bynum, Janie. *Nutmeg and Barley: A Budding Friendship.* Candlewick Press, 2006. Neighbors Nutmeg the squirrel and Barley the mouse believe that they have nothing in common until an emergency forces them to discover surprising things about each other.

Carlson, Nancy L. *I Don't Like to Read!* Viking, 2007. Henry the mouse likes everything about first grade except reading, but with help from school and home, he is delightfully surprised. See also *First Grade, Here I Come!*

Chaconas, Dori. *Christmas Mouseling.* Illustrated by Susan Kathleen Hartung. Viking, 2005. When her shivering baby is born on a winter night, a mouse follows some animals to a special manger.

Currey, Anna. *Truffle's Christmas.* Orchard Books, 2000. An unselfish little mouse has his Christmas wishes fulfilled by Santa.

Dunbar, Joyce. *Where's My Sock?* Illustrated by Sanja Rescek. Chicken House/Scholastic, 2006. Pippin the mouse and Tog the cat leave no drawer unturned as they search for Pippin's missing "yellow sock with clocks."

Fagan, Cary. *Ten Old Men and a Mouse.* Illustrated by Gary Clement. Tundra Books, 2007. The synagogue was once a busy, bustling place, but now only ten old men come to tend it and pray each day. Then one day, a little scritch-scratch betrays the first new member in years: a tiny mouse who has taken up residence among the holy books.

Goodrich, Carter. *A Creature Was Stirring.* Illustrated by Carter Goodrich. Simon & Schuster Books for Young Readers, 2006. Based on the original poem by Clement C. Moore, a young mouse is unable to sleep in anticipation of Christmas.

Henkes, Kevin. *Lilly's Big Day.* Greenwillow Books, 2006. When her teacher announces that he is getting married, Lilly the mouse sets her heart on being the flower girl at his wedding.

Henkes, Kevin. *Wemberly Worried.* Greenwillow Books, 2000. Wemberly the mouse worries about everything, including the first day of nursery school.

Moss, Miriam. *Smudge's Grumpy Day.* Illustrated by Lynne Chapman. Gingham Dog Press, 2007. Smudge the mouse gets up on the wrong side of the bed, but she soon figures out how to deal with a grumpy day.

Noonan, Julia. *Mouse by Mouse: A Counting Adventure.* Dutton, 2003. Humorous illustrations depict a lonely mouse and his growing company.

Numeroff, Laura J. *If You Take a Mouse to School.* Illustrated by Felicia Bond. Laura Geringer Books, 2002. Taking a mouse to school can lead to a series of consequences. One of several Numeroff books, including *If You Take a Mouse to the Movies* and *If You Give a Mouse a Cookie*.

Ormerod, Jan. *Miss Mouse's Day*. HarperCollins, 2001. A mouse's day includes all sorts of activities and finishes with a goodnight kiss.

Polushkin, Maria. *Mother, Mother, I Want Another*. Illustrated by Jon Goodell. Knopf, 2005. Anxious to get her son to sleep, Mrs. Mouse tries to find exactly what he wants.

Provencher, Rose-Marie. *Mouse Cleaning*. Illustrated by Bernadette Pons. Henry Holt & Company, 2001. A woman is inspired to house clean when she discovers a mouse in her house.

Reid, Barbara. *The Subway Mouse*. Scholastic, 2005. A little mouse who lives deep in a subway station learns to stand up for himself.

Sacre, Antonio. *The Barking Mouse*. Illustrated by Alfredo Aguirre. Albert Whitman, 2003. A brave mother mouse saves her family when she frightens a cat away.

Schneider, Antonie. *The Dearest Little Mouse in the World*. Illustrated by Quentin Grébin. North-South Books, 2003. A little mouse ignores a barking dog until one day she sees the dog in a different light.

Thompson, Lauren. *Mouse's First Spring*. Illustrated by Buket Erdogan. Simon & Schuster, 2005. A mouse and its mother experience the delights of nature on a windy spring day.

Waber, Bernard. *The Mouse that Snored*. Houghton Mifflin, 2000. A snoring mouse wakens the residents of a quiet house.

Wallace, Nancy Elizabeth, and Linda K. Friedlaender. *Look! Look! Look!* Marshall Cavendish Children, 2006. Three mice "borrow" a postcard that is a reproduction of a painting, and from it they learn about color, pattern, line, and shape. Includes instructions for making and sending a postcard.

Walsh, Ellen Stoll. *Mouse Shapes*. Harcourt, 2007. Three mice make a variety of things out of shapes. A companion to *Mouse Paint*.

Wormell, Christopher. *George and the Dragon*. Knopf, 2006. George the mouse unintentionally rids the kingdom of a ferocious dragon.

Poems

"In Minot, North Dakota" in *The Frogs Wore Red Suspenders* by Jack Prelutsky. Illustrated by Petra Mathers. Greenwillow Books, 2002.

"Mary Had a Little Mouse" in *Peter, Peter, Pizza-Eater and Other Silly Rhymes* by Bruce Lansky. Illustrated by Stephen Carpenter. Meadowbrook Press, 2006.

"Mouse" in *The Llama Who Had No Pajama: 100 Favorite Poems* by Mary Ann Hoberman. Illustrated by Betty Fraser. Harcourt, 2006.

"Three Kind Mice" in *Mary Had a Little Jam and Other Silly Rhymes* by Bruce Lansky. Illustrated by Stephen Carpenter. Meadowbrook Creations, 2004.

"Hickory Dickory Dock" (nursery rhyme)
Hickory Dickory Dock,
The mouse ran up the clock.
The clock struck one,
The mouse came down.
Hickory Dickory Dock!

Alphabet Activities

ABC Connect-the-Dots

Copy one pattern on page 129 for each child. Have the children connect the dots from A to Z to find the mystery picture.

Dream Cheese Alphabet

Enlarge and copy one each of the patterns on pages 130–131 for each child. Have the children color the mouse and pieces of cheese and cut out the cheese pieces. The children can match the alphabet cheese pieces to the appropri-

ate spot by the mouse then glue them in place.

Creative Activities

Paper Plate Mouse

Copy one mouse face for each child from page 132. Have the children color in the faces and cut them out. Give each child a paper plate and have each child glue the face to the plate. Cut a second paper plate in half for each child. Attach two halves to each plate for mouse ears.

Mouse Cookies

Chocolate chip cookies may be served if the book *If You Give a Mouse a Cookie* is read.

Tube Mouse

Make a mouse with a toilet paper roll. Glue on large circles for ears, and a piece of yarn for the tail. Cover the front end with a large circle, and have the children draw faces on their mice.

Pear Mice Snack

Place one canned pear half on a small plate. Add almond slivers for ears (if there are no nut allergies in the group), raisins for eyes, and licorice for tail and whiskers.

Cheese

Everyone knows that mice love cheese. Bring in a few varieties of cheese and have the children sample. Be on the alert for dairy allergies.

Creating Mice Characters

Make five mice.

- Trace the mouse pattern onto gray fun foam.
- Trace the ear patterns onto pink fun foam.
- Cut out all the pieces.
- Glue the ears in place on the mouse.
- Apply whiskers and a mouth using black fabric paint.
- Apply two teeth using white fabric paint.
- Glue on a small pink pom pom over the whiskers for a nose.
- Glue on two medium-sized roly eyes.
- Glue velcro to back.

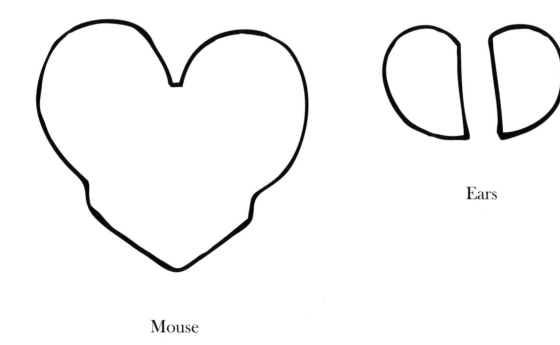

Mouse

Ears

_ ouse

A B C D E F G H I J K L M N O P Q R S T U V W X Y Z

Dream Cheese Patterns

Paper Plate Mouse

M M M M M M M M M

M ------------------------------- M

m m m m m m m m

m ------------------------------- m

Mm Mm Mm Mm

Mm ----------------------------- Mm

n – nest

Introduction

A nest theme can be nicely linked with eggs and birds, or used with springtime programs. The "n" sound is popular, and thus important to learn.

Introductory Poem

It starts with "n" and ends with "est."
For birds, a home like it is best.

Finger Play Speller

- Use the finger play glove following the pattern and instructions on pages 13–16.

- Make one each of n, e, s, t for the glove using the patterns on pages 17–18.

- Make one nest finger play character using the pattern on page 136.

- Affix the nest finger play character in the center velcro tab of the glove.

- One by one, attach the n, e, s, t letters onto the glove. Pause between each one, focusing on the sounds and the blends: n ne nes nest. Once "nest" has been achieved, spell the word by pointing to the letters and saying them out loud.

Name Game

- Have the children think of the name of a person that begins with "n" (Nellie, Ned, Nanette, etc.).

- Have children work on sentences that focus on the "n" sound (Nancy nods at her new nest. Ned neatly knit nine noodles. Etc.). Make the sentences as silly as possible.

Finger Plays

- Make five of the nest finger play character, using the pattern and instructions on page 136.

- Practice rhyming sounds with the finger plays. Use the ones provided, or look for others. Use the finger play characters to count either up or down with the plays.

Count Down Rhyme

"Five Empty Nests" (Sung to the tune "Five Bran Muffins" on *Sidewalk Shuffle*. Sandra Beech. A&M Records, 1984.)

Five empty nests in a maple tree.

Five empty nests crying, "please pick me."

A bird came looking for a nest one day.

She picked an empty nest and decided to stay.

Count Up Rhyme

"One Little Nest"

One little nest on a branch in a tree.

With one mama bird, lonely as can be.

A birdie flying by landed in the tree.

She built another nest, and kept her company.

Resources for Storytime

Use some of these books and poems, or any of your favorites, to create a well-rounded storytime program.

Books

Asch, Frank. *Baby Bird's First Nest.* Harcourt Brace, 1999. Baby Bird falls from her nest and, with the help of Frog, makes her way back to the nest.

Engelbreit, Mary. *Queen of Easter.* HarperCollins, 2006. Ann Estelle is not impressed with her new Easter hat until a robin lays eggs in it.

Minshull, Evelyn. *Eaglet's World.* Illustrated by Andrea Gabriel. Albert Whitman, 2002. A young eaglet hesitates to leave the comfort of his parents' nest.

Napoli, Donna Jo. *Albert.* Illustrated by Jim LaMarche. Silver Whistle/Harcourt Brace, 2001. Two cardinals come to build a nest in Albert's hand.

Nicholls, Judith. *Billywise.* Illustrated by Jason Cockcroft. Bloomsbury Children's Books, 2002. The night finally arrives when Billywise the owlet, guided by his mother, jumps from the nest and flies.

Rockwell, Anne. *Two Blue Jays.* Illustrated by Megan Halsey. Walker & Co., 2003. A classroom of children get a front-row view as a pair of blue jays build a nest.

Ruurs, Margriet. *In My Backyard.* Illustrated by Ron Broda. Tundra, 2007. From the singing of little wrens to the paper wasps building their nests, this book celebrates the backyard habitat.

Stone, Susan. *The Nest.* Illustrated by Xiangyi Mo & Jingwen Wang. Shortland, 2003. Part of the Storyteller Series.

Poems

"The Bird's Nest" in *100 Best Poems for Children.* Edited by Roger McGough. Illustrated by Sheila Moxley. Puffin, 2002.

"In Winnemucca" in *The Frogs Wore Red Suspenders* by Jack Prelutsky. Illustrated by Petra Mathers. Greenwillow Books, 2002.

"Nellie's Wee Nest"

Nellie the nuthatcher built a wee nest,

To hatch a small egg or two.

Nellie was in for a challenging test,

When instead she laid thirty-two!

Alphabet Activities

ABC Connect-the-Dots

Copy one pattern on page 137 for each child. Have the children connect the dots from A to Z to find the mystery picture.

Alphabet Nest

Enlarge and copy one each of the patterns on pages 138–139 for each child. Have the children color the bird and the pieces of nest and cut out the nest pieces. The children can match the alphabet nest pieces to the appropriate spot on the nest then glue them in place.

Creative Activities

Bird's Nest Craft

Give each child a base for a nest (a margarine lid works well). Have the children add shredded brown paper to the base to make a nest. Add two or three malted candy eggs to the nest, or have the children draw and cut paper eggs. Optionally the children can add a bird.

Edible Nests

Have children make their own delicious nests with coconut and a thick icing glaze. You may wish to add jellybeans or candy eggs.

Nest Identification

After the birds have left, collect a few types of nests. Have the children examine the nests and learn which type of bird built that nest. Reference books on nests would show pictures of many types of nests.

Play-dough Nests

Using a garlic press or a stringer, make long strings of brown play-dough. Have the children arrange the strings into a nest.

Creating Nest Characters

Make five nests.

- Enlarge and trace the nest pattern (below) onto brown fun foam.

- Cut out all the pieces.

- Apply the nest details with brown fabric paint. Alternatively, glue scraps of brown yarn to nest.

- Glue velcro to back.

_est

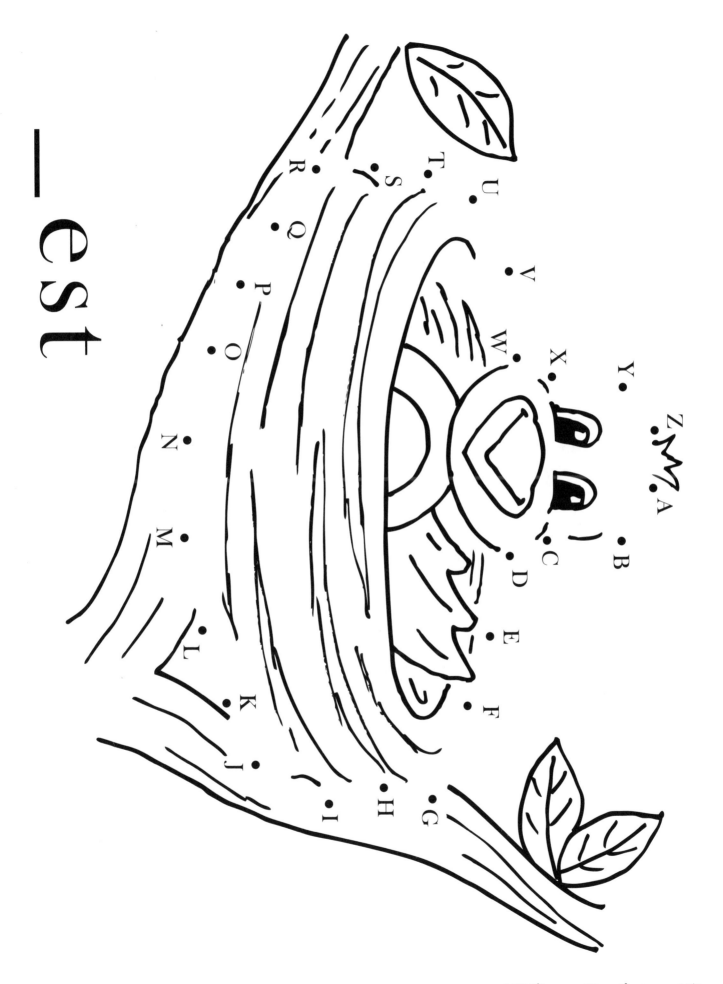

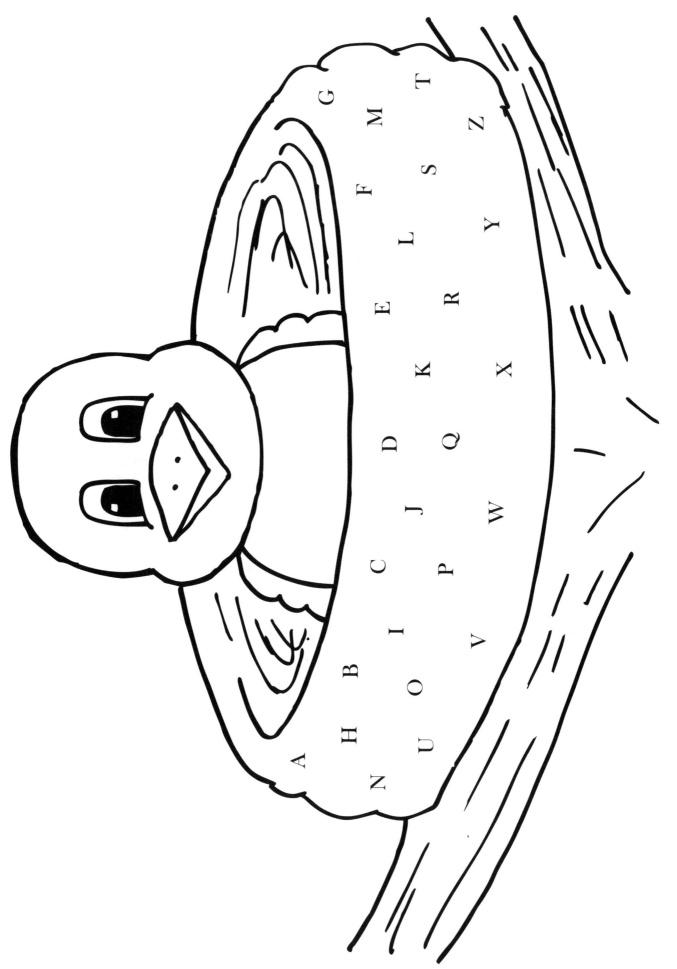

Alphabet Nest Pattern

N N N N N N N N N N N

N - - - - - - - - - - - - - - - N

n n n n n n n n n n n

n - - - - - - - - - - - - - - - n

Nn Nn Nn Nn Nn Nn

Nn - - - - - - - - - - - - - Nn

O — Owl

Introduction

Owls can be used in a variety of programs. There is sufficient material available to do a program specifically on owls, or you may choose to incorporate into other themes such as birds, night, Halloween, or sounds. The "whoo" sound of owls is a good blend practice, while the short "o" sound is essential to learn. The long "o" sound can be practiced later with words such as "rope" and "bowl."

Introductory Poem

She starts with "ow" and ends with "l." And "whoo, whoo" is the sound she'll howl.

Finger Play Speller

- Use the finger play glove following the pattern and instructions on pages 13–16.
- Make one each of o, w, l for the glove using the patterns on pages 17–18.

- Make one owl finger play character using the pattern on page 145.
- Affix the owl finger play character in the center velcro tab of the glove.
- One by one, attach the o, w, l letters onto the glove. Pause between each one, focusing on the sounds and the blends: o ow owl. Once "owl" has been achieved, spell the word by pointing to the letters and saying them out loud.

Name Game

- Have the children think of the name of a person that begins with "o" (Oliver, Oscar, Olivia, etc.).
- Have children work on sentences that focus on the "o" sound (Oliver owl overheard Oscar howl. Olivia openly objects to owls. Etc.). Make the sentences as silly as possible.

Finger Plays

- Make five of the owl finger play character using the pattern and instructions on page 145.

- Practice rhyming sounds with the finger plays. Use the ones provided, or look for others. Use the finger play characters to count either up or down with the plays.

Count Up Rhyme

"One Night Owl" (Sung to the tune "She'll be Coming 'Round the Mountain.")

There was one night owl in the tree: WHO, WHO!

There was one night owl in the tree: WHO, WHO!

Oh, he called up to the sky to an owl flying by.

And the owl came and joined him happily: WHO, WHO!

(Repeat for 2, 3, 4)

Count Up Rhyme

"One Little Owl"

One little owl with a who, who, who
Called for a friend, and then there were two.

Two little owls, perched up in a tree
Called for a friend, and then there were three.

Three little owls by the barnyard door
Called for a friend, and then there were four.

Four little owls, one more to arrive
Called for a friend, and then there were five.

Resources for Storytime

Use some of these books and poems, or any of your favorites, to create a well-rounded storytime program.

Books

Brown, Alan. *Hoot and Holler.* Illustrated by Rimantras Rolia. Knopf, 2001. Two owls separated by a storm discover their true feelings for each other.

Brown, Richard. *The Moonlit Owl.* Cambridge University Press, 2003. One of a series of British books, this one being a trip out in the moonlight.

Brunelle, Nicholas. *Snow Moon.* Viking, 2005. One wintry night, a child awakens to find at his window a mysterious owl that takes the child on a journey.

Gibbons, Joyce. *The Little Brown Owl and Me.* Illustrated by Jane Lenoir. Coastal Publishing, 2001. A little boy who is lost in the woods finds his way home thanks to an owl.

Hutchins, Pat. *Good Night Owl.* Aladdin, 1990. Owl can't sleep because of his noisy forest friends.

Johansen, Hanna. *The Duck and the Owl.* Illustrated by Kathi Bhend. David R.

Godine, 2005. A duck and an owl contemplate starting a friendship, despite their differences in appearance and behavior.

Nicholls, Judith. *Billywise*. Illustrated by Jason Cockcroft. Bloomsbury Children's Books, 2002. The night finally arrives when Billywise the owlet, guided by his mother, jumps from the nest and flies.

Runton, Andy. *Owly: Flying Lessons*. Top Shelf Productions, 2005. Owly tries to figure out why he can't fly. See others in this series.

Slingsby, Janet. *Hush-a-bye Babies*. Illustrated by Andy Beckett. Barron's, 2001. Baby owls at bedtime.

Spruling, Margaret. *Bilby Moon*. Illustrated by Danny Snell. Kane-Miller, 2001. Bilby greets the moon every night, but one night a piece of the moon is missing, and he sets out to find the piece.

Thaler, Mike. *Owly*. Illustrated by David Wiesner. Walker & Co., 2002. When Owly asks his mother question after question about the world, she finds ways to answer his requests.

Tomlinson, Jill. *The Owl Who Was Afraid of the Dark*. Illustrated by Paul Howard. Candlewick Press, 2001. A mommy owl teaches her frightened little one the pleasures of the evening.

Waddell, Martin. *Owl Babies*. Illustrated by Patrick Benson. Candlewick Press, 2002. Three owl babies wait for their mother's return.

Wilson, Karma. *Bear's New Friend*. Illustrated by Jane Chapman. Margaret K. McElderry Books, 2006. Bear and his friends persuade a bashful owl to play with them.

Yolen, Jane. *Owl Moon*. Illustrated by John Schoenherr. Philomel Books, 2002. On a winter's night under a full moon a father and daughter go into the woods to see a great horned owl.

Poems

"One Old Owl" in *The Frogs Wore Red Suspenders*. Jack Prelutsky. Illustrated by Petra Mathers. Greenwillow Books, 2002.

"Owl" in *Wake Up, Sleepy Head!: Early Morning Poems* by Mandy Ross. Illustrated by Dubravka Kolanovic. Child's Play, 2004.

"Owl Song." in *A Pizza the Size of the Sun: Poems* by Jack Prelutsky. Drawings by James Stevenson. Greenwillow Books, 1996.

"Owl Grammar"

"Mother," said wee owl, "tell me, please do: Why do we owls have to say who?" There's grammar for humans, and for owls too.

Whom is for humans.

While who is for you.

Alphabet Activities

ABC Connect-the-Dots

Copy one pattern on page 146 for each child. Have the children connect the dots from A to Z to find the mystery picture.

ABC Owl

Enlarge and copy one each of the patterns on pages 147–148 for each child. Have the children color the owl and the owl feathers and cut out the feathers. The children can match the alphabet feathers to the appropriate spot on the owl then glue them in place.

Creative Activities

Owl Ornament

Enlarge and copy one owl pattern on page 145 for each child from a heavier material such as Bristol board or construction paper. Have the children color and cut all the pieces. Attach the wings by placing them behind the owl pattern and securing them with paper fasteners. Spread the paper fasteners through the center of the owl's eyes. Tie a small piece of string through the top of the owl to hang him from a branch.

Owl in a Tree

Cut a hole along the lower part of a toilet paper roll. The hole should be large enough to comfortably fit a child's finger. Around the hole have the children draw a tree trunk with branches. Give each child a small drawing of an owl face. Have the child tape the face on the pointer finger. When the child pokes the pointer finger through the toilet paper roll, it looks like an owl in a tree.

Thumbprint Owls

Using washable ink, have each child put their thumbprint on a small piece of paper. Have each child glue on roly eyes and draw beaks to create owls.

Owl Masks

Make owl masks using paper plates for the face and construction paper for the beaks. You may also wish to have children glue feathers on the top of the mask.

Owl Gingerbread Cookies

Make owl cookies with a special cutter, but use a gingerbread recipe instead of shortbread. The owls will have a nicer coloring.

Creating Owl Characters

Make five owls.

- Trace the owl pattern onto dark brown fun foam.
- Trace the chest pattern onto light brown fun foam.
- Cut out all the pieces.
- Glue on two large roly eyes.
- Glue the chest piece onto the owl.
- Apply the beak and feet using yellow fabric paint.
- Glue velcro to back.

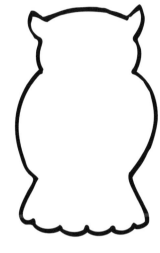

Chest

Owl

Owl Ornament Pattern

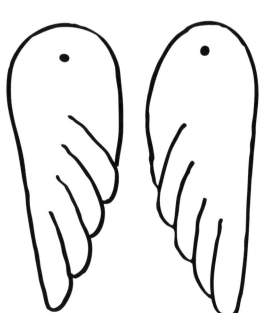

__ w l

Feather Patterns

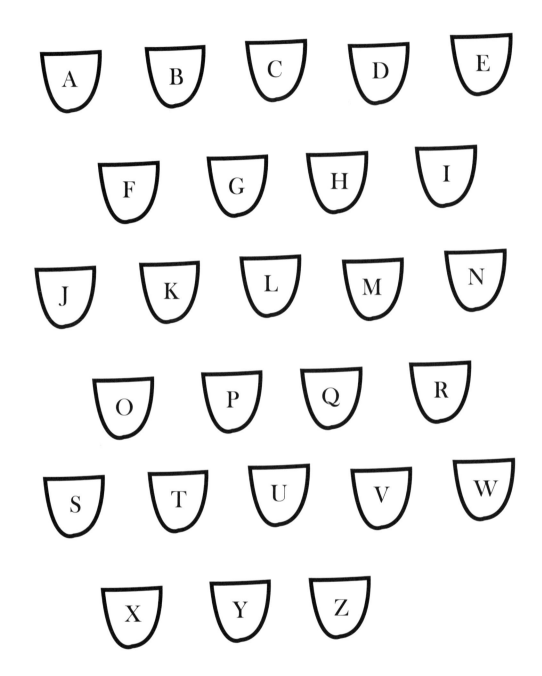

P — Pig

Introduction

Children are fascinated by most farm animals, but they seem especially drawn to cows and pigs. Maybe it is because of the unusual sounds they make, or maybe it is simply their appearance. Either way, a pig program is bound to be a hit in any season. Practice the "p" sound patiently in the program.

Introductory Poem

She starts with "p" and ends with "ig." She goes "oink, oink" and is quite big.

Finger Play Speller

- Use the finger play glove following the pattern and instructions on pages 13–16.

- Make one each of p, i, g for the glove using the patterns on pages 17–18.

- Make one pig finger play character using the patterns on page 154.

- Affix the pig finger play character in the center velcro tab of the glove.

- One by one, attach the p, i, g letters onto the glove. Pause between each one, focusing on the sounds and the blends: p pi pig. Once "pig" has been achieved, spell the word by pointing to the letters and saying them out loud.

Name Game

- Have the children think of the name of a person that begins with "p" (Polly, Percy, Penelope, etc.).

- Have children work on sentences that focus on the "p" sound (Percy the pig pokes at produce. Penelope Park is partial to pancakes. Etc.). Make the sentences as silly as possible.

Finger Plays

- Make five of the pig finger play character, using the pattern and instructions on page 154.

- Practice rhyming sounds with the finger plays. Use the ones provided, or look for others. Use the finger play characters to count either up or down with the plays.

Count Down Rhyme

"Five Pink Piggies" (Sung to the tune "Five Brown Teddies" in *Oranges and Lemons*. Karen King. Illustrated by Ian Beck. Oxford, 1985.)

Five pink piggies, wiggling in the mud.
Five pink piggies, wiggling in the mud.
If one pink piggy falls down with a "thud."
There'd be four pink piggies, wiggling in the mud.

(Repeat for 4, 3, 2, 1)

Stay and Play Rhyme

"This Little Piggy" (Traditional)
This little piggy went to market,
This little piggy stayed home.
This little piggy had roast beef,
This little piggy had none.
This little piggy cried, "WEE WEE WEE!" all the way home.

Resources for Storytime

Use some of these books and poems, or any of your favorites, to create a well-rounded storytime program.

Books

Addy, Sharon Hart. *Lucky Jake.* Illustrated by Wade Zahares. Houghton Mifflin, 2006. While panning for gold with his Pa, Jake adopts a pig that he names Dog.

Ashman, Linda. *Can You Make a Piggy Giggle?* Illustrated by Henry Cole. Dutton Children's Books, 2002. Rhymed suggestions for making a pig giggle.

Bailey, Linda. *Goodnight, Sweet Pig.* Illustrated by Josée Masse. Kids Can Press, 2007. Pig number one is trying to sleep while other active pigs are counted. A rhyming text.

Brantford, Henrietta. *Little Pig Figwort Can't Get to Sleep.* Illustrated by Claudio Muñoz. Clarion Books, 2000. Little Pig Figwort can't sleep so he goes off to the North Pole, the moon, and the bottom of the sea.

Brown, Margaret Wise. *The Good Little Bad Little Pig.* Illustrated by Dan Yaccarino. Hyperion Books for Children, 2002. Peter's wish comes true when he gets a little pet pig who is sometimes good and sometimes bad.

Carlson, Nancy L. *Get Up and Go!* Viking, 2006. Piggy characters encourage readers to turn off the television and get active.

Christelow, Eileen. *The Great Pig Search.* Clarion Books, 2001. Bert and Ethel go to Florida to look for their runaway pigs and find them in surprising places.

Faulkner, Keith. *Piggy's Belly Button.* Illustrated by Jonathan Lambert. Random House, 2003. Piggy's mother warns him not to push his belly button, but he doesn't listen.

Fox, Christyan, and Diane Fox. *Pirate PiggyWiggy*. Handprint Books, 2003. PiggyWiggy embarks on an imaginary sailing adventure. See also *Fire Fighter PiggyWiggy* and *Astronaut PiggyWiggy*.

Frantz, Jennifer. *Wilbur Finds a Friend*. Illustrated by Aleksey and Olga Ivanov. HarperCollins, 2006. Wilbur is scared about moving to the Zuckerman farm, but makes a friend after he arrives. A beginning reader based on the novel.

Jones, Melanie Davis. *Pigs Rock*. Illustrated by Bob Staake. Viking, 2003. A music band of pigs play various kinds of music for their fans.

Martin, David. *Piggy and Dad Go Fishing*. Illustrated by Frank Remkiewicz. Scholastic, 2005. When his dad takes Piggy fishing for the first time and Piggy ends up feeling sorry for the worms and the fish, they decide to make some changes.

McLarey, Kristina Thermaenius. *When You Take a Pig to a Party*. Illustrated by Marjory Wunsch. Orchard Books, 2000. Havoc ensues when a pig is taken to a friend's birthday party.

McPhail, David. *Piggy's Pancake Parlor*. Dutton Children's Books, 2002. Piggy and Fox open a restaurant where they serve special pancakes. See also *Pigs Aplenty, Pigs Galore!* and *Pigs Ahoy!*

Numeroff, Laura Joffe. *If You Give a Pig a Party*. Illustrated by Felicia Bond. Laura Geringer Books, 2005. One thing leads to another when you give a pig a party. See also *If You Give a Pig a Pancake*, 1998.

Rand, Gloria. *Little Flower*. Illustrated by R. W. Alley. Henry Holt & Company, 2002. When Miss Pearl falls and breaks her hip, her potbellied pig goes for help.

Roche, Denis. *Little Pig Is Capable*. Houghton Mifflin, 2002. Little Pig's parents worry about him to an unusual degree.

Saltzberg, Barney. *Cornelius P. Mud, are you Ready for School?* Candlewick Press, 2007. Cornelius the pig has his own style when preparing for school in the morning, but he does not really feel ready until he gets a kiss.

Thaler, Mike. *Pig Little*. Illustrated by Paige Miglio. Henry Holt & Company, 2006. The story of a little pig's adventures, set in poetic form.

Tryon, Leslie. *Patsy Says*. Atheneum Books for Young Readers, 2001. Patsy Pig is determined to teach Ms. Klingensmith's class some manners.

Van Leeuwen, Jean. *Amanda Pig and the Really Hot Day*. Illustrated by Ann Schweninger. Dial Books for Young Readers, 2005. Amanda Pig and her family and friends try to find different ways to beat the heat. (A Beginning Reader.)

Whatley, Bruce. *Wait! No Paint!* HarperCollins, 2001. The three little pigs get a little mixed up with the help of a mysterious voice.

Wild, Margaret. *Piglet and Papa*. Abrams Books for Young Readers, 2007. When Piglet's beloved father chases her away after she plays too rough, all of the barnyard animals try to make her feel better, but Piglet is still afraid that her father no longer loves her.

Winthrop, Elizabeth. *Dumpy La Rue*. Illustrated by Betsy Lewin. Henry Holt & Company, 2001. A rhyming story about a pig who loves to dance.

Poems

"Little Pig's Treat" in *Falling Up*. Shel Silverstein. HarperCollins, 1996.

"Pig" in *Wake Up, Sleepy Head!: Early Morning Poems* by Mandy Ross. Illustrated by Dubravka Kolanovic. Child's Play, 2004.

"Pignic" in *Bear Hugs: Romantically Ridiculous Animal Rhymes* by Karma Wilson. Illustrated by Suzanne Watts. Margaret K. McElderry Books, 2005.

"To Market, To Market"
(Traditional)
To market, to market to buy a fat pig.
Home again, home again, jiggety jig.
To market, to market to buy a fat hog.
Home again, home again, jiggety jog.

Alphabet Activities

ABC Connect-the-Dots

Copy one pattern on page 155 for each child. Have the children connect the dots from A to Z to find the mystery picture.

Truffle Alphabet

Enlarge and copy one each of the patterns on pages 156–157 for each child. Have the children color the pig and the truffles and cut out the truffles. The children can match the alphabet truffles to the appropriate spot on the pig sheet then glue them in place.

Creative Activities

Pig Tails

Have the children curl pink pipe cleaners around pencils until tight curls are obtained. Once removed from the pencils, the tails hold their shape. The children can fasten the tails to a back belt loop, or the tails can be pinned onto clothing.

Pig Snouts

Cut one pocket from an egg carton for each child. Fasten string to both sides of each pocket. Have each child draw and color the snout. Fasten in place with string.

Snorting Contest

Give children the opportunity to practice their "oinks" and "snorts." Have prizes for everybody, especially for the loudest, snortiest, silliest, etc.

Pig Snout Snack

Serve pig snouts by decorating plain round shortbread cookies with two dabs of icing.

Creating Pig Characters

Make five pigs.

- Trace pig pattern onto pink fun foam.
- Cut out all the pieces.
- Glue on small roly eye.
- Curl small piece of pipe cleaner into a curly shape and glue to pig to make tail.
- Apply mouth and snout using fabric paint.
- Glue velcro to back.

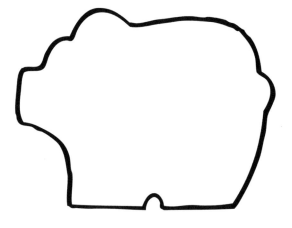

Pig

_ig

Truffle Alphabet Patterns

P P P P P P P P P P P

P   P

p p p p p p p p p p p

p   p

Pp Pp Pp Pp Pp Pp

Pp   Pp

Q — Quilt

Introduction

Snowy, blowy evenings and a warm quilt—instantly an image is conjured. Children can learn about patchwork and fabrics with this theme. The "qu" blend is clearly portrayed with this theme.

Introductory Poem

It starts with "qu" and ends with "ilt"
From scraps of fabric it is built.

Finger Play Speller

- Use the finger play glove following the pattern and instructions on pages 13–16.

- Make one each of q, u, i, l, t for the glove using the patterns on pages 17–18.

- Make one quilt finger play character using the pattern on page 163.

- Affix the quilt finger play character in the center velcro tab of the glove.

- One by one, attach the q, u, i, l, t letters onto the glove. Pause between each one, focusing on the sounds and the blends: q qu qui quil quilt. Once "quilt" has been achieved, spell the word by pointing to the letters and saying them out loud.

Name Game

- Have the children think of the name of a person that begins with "q" (Quentin, Queenie, Quaker, etc.).

- Have children work on sentences that focus on the "qu" sound (Quentin questions the quality of quilts. Queenie's quacker has quivering quills. Etc.). Make the sentences as silly as possible.

Finger Plays

- Make five of the quilt finger play character, using the pattern and instructions on page 163.

- Practice rhyming sounds with the finger plays. Use the ones provided, or look for others. Use the finger play characters to count either up or down with the plays.

Count Down Rhyme

"Five Quilts"

(Sung to the tune "Five Little Frogs" ["Five Green and Speckled Frogs"] on *Singable Songs for the Very Young*. Raffi. Troubadour Records, 1976.)

Five quilts on Mama's bed:
Yellow, green and blue and red,
Covering bottom up to top.
The sun shone down that day,
Mama put a quilt away
Then there were four quilts left atop.

Repeat for 4, 3, 2, 1

Count Up Rhyme

"One Little Quilt"

One little quilt, hand stitched through and through
Mama made another one—that made two.

Two little quilts, made at a quilting bee
Grandma made another one—that made three.

Three little quilts, by the bedroom door
Sister made another one—that made four.

Four little quilts, with colors so alive
Auntie made another one—that made five.

Resources for Storytime

Use some of these books and poems, or any of your favorites, to create a well-rounded storytime program.

Books

Atkins, Jeannie. *A Name on the Quilt*. Illustrated by Tad Hills. Simon & Schuster, 2003. The death of a beloved uncle sparks family to gather together to make a panel for the AIDS Memorial Quilt.

Bild, Linda A. *Grandpa's Quilt*. Sagebrush, 2000. A Rookie Reader.

Brumbeau, Jeff. *The Quiltmaker's Journey*. Illustrated by Gail de Marcken. Orchard Books, 2005. A young girl makes the loveliest quilts in the land, and decides to give them away. See also *The Quiltmaker's Gift*.

Cline-Ransome, Lesa. *Quilt Counting*. Illustrated by James E. Ransome. SeaStar Books, 2002. Rhyming text follows the numbers from one to ten and back again to describe how a special family quilt is made in a country farmhouse.

Flournoy, Valerie. *The Patchwork Quilt*. Illustrated by Jerry Pinkney. Dial, 2001. Three generations of women make a story quilt together, telling their family's life.

Gibbons, Gail. *The Quilting Bee.* HarperCollins, 2004. An introduction to quilt making, including a history of the craft.

Good, Merle. *Reuben and the Quilt.* Faithworks, 2005. An Amish family decides to work together to make a quilt to raise funds for a sick neighbor.

Hoberman, Mary Ann. *I'm Going to Grandma's.* Illustrated by Tiphanie Beeke. Harcourt, 2007. A special quilt keeps a little girl from feeling homesick while sleeping over with her grandparents.

Hopkinson, Deborah. *Under the Quilt of Night.* Illustrated by James E. Ransome. Aladdin, 2005. A slave girl on the run sees a quilt with a center square made of deep blue fabric and recognizes it as a signal from friends on the Underground Railroad.

Hopkinson, Deborah. *Sweet Clara and the Freedom Quilt.* Illustrated by James Ransome. Knopf, 2003. A slave begins to save scraps of colored cloth for a quilt that becomes a map depicting the route of the Underground Railroad.

Johnston, Tony. *Quilt Story.* Illustrated by Tomie de Paola. Puffin, 2002. A girl discovers years later a quilt her mother had made for her and continues to work on it.

Kinsey-Warnock, Natalie. *Canada Geese Quilt.* Illustrated by Leslie W. Bowman. Dutton, 2001. Ariel and her grandmother work together to create a quilt for the new baby.

Kurtz, Shirley. *The Boy and the Quilt (Fun on the Road).* Illustrated by Cheryl Benner. Good Books, 2002. A little boy makes a quilt of his own with help from his mother and sister. Includes instructions for making a quilt.

Paul, Ann. *Eight Hands Round: A Patchwork Alphabet.* Illustrated by Jeanette Winter. HarperCollins, 1996. Introduces the letters of the alphabet with names of early American patchwork quilt patterns.

Paulsen, Gary. *The Quilt.* Random House, 2004. A young boy goes to live with his grandmother during World War II.

Polacco, Patricia. *Keeping Quilt.* Aladdin, 2001. A quilt is passed down through a family and is incorporated into the lives of the family members over time.

Porter, Connie. *Addy's Wedding Quilt.* Pleasant Company Publications, 2001. Addy's wedding present to her parents and her family's past is made fun of.

Ringgold, Faith. *Cassie's Word Quilt.* Dragonfly Books, 2004. Quilt motifs abound in the illustrations as Cassie tours her home and neighborhood. See also *Tar Beach.*

Root, Phyllis. *The Name Quilt.* Farrar, Straus and Giroux, 2003. A young girl hears family stories while tucked in underneath a family name quilt.

Van Leeuwen, Jean. *Papa and the Pioneer Quilt.* Illustrated by Rebecca Bond. Dial Books for Young Readers, 2007. As her family travels by wagon train to Oregon, a young girl gathers scraps of cloth to make a quilt.

Woodson, Jacqueline. *Show Way.* Illustrated by Hudson Talbott. Putnam, 2005. The making of "Show Ways," or quilts which once served as secret maps for freedom-seeking slaves, is a tradition passed from mother to daughter in the author's family.

Poems

Hines, Anna Grossnickle. *Pieces: A Year in Poems and Quilts.* HarperCollins, 2003.

"The Plumpuppets" by Christopher Morley in *A Family of Poems: My Favorite Poetry for Children* compiled by Caroline Kennedy. Illustrated by Jon Muth. Hyperion, 2005.

"Queenie the Quilter"

Queenie the quilter crafted a quilt
A quilt of exceptional quality
Querying couples inquired of her
If she could make quilts in more quantity.

Alphabet Activities

ABC Connect-the-Dots

Copy one pattern on page 164 for each child. Have the children connect the dots from A to Z to find the mystery picture.

ABC Patchwork Quilt

Enlarge and copy one each of the patterns on pages 165–166 for each child. Have the children color the bed and the quilt pieces and cut out the quilt pieces. The children can match the alphabet quilt pieces to the appropriate spot on the bed then glue them in place.

Creative Activities

Cutting Quilt Shapes

Cutting shapes from fabric is more difficult than from paper. Using templates of circles, triangles, squares, and rectangles, have the children draw the shapes onto fabric and then cut them out.

Quilt Lacing

Make patchwork squares from bristol board. Using a hole punch, make holes around the perimeter of each square. Give each child a plastic needle and yarn and have them lace the sides of the quilt block. For fun you might try to have them lace their squares together to form a quilt.

A Quilted "Q"

Make one letter "q" from construction paper for each child. Have the children tear colored paper or fabric scraps into small pieces. The children can cover their own letter with "quilt scraps."

Quilt Hopscotch

Using pieces of bristol board, make squares for hopscotch. Have the children decorate the squares like patchwork pieces. Arrange the squares into a hopscotch formation and securely fasten the squares to the floor. Let the children have fun playing the game.

Creating Quilt Characters

Make five quilts.

- Trace the quilt pattern onto any color of fun foam.
- Cut out all the pieces.
- Cut several small squares of fun foam in various colors.
- Glue assorted squares onto the quilt.
- Apply stitches between squares using black fabric paint.
- Glue velcro to back.

Quilt

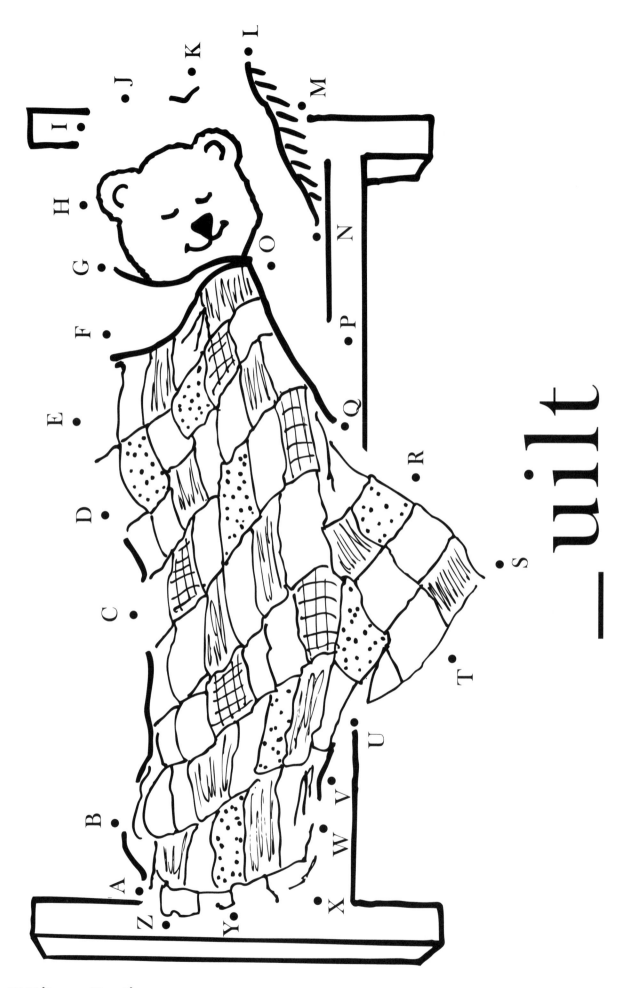

_uilt

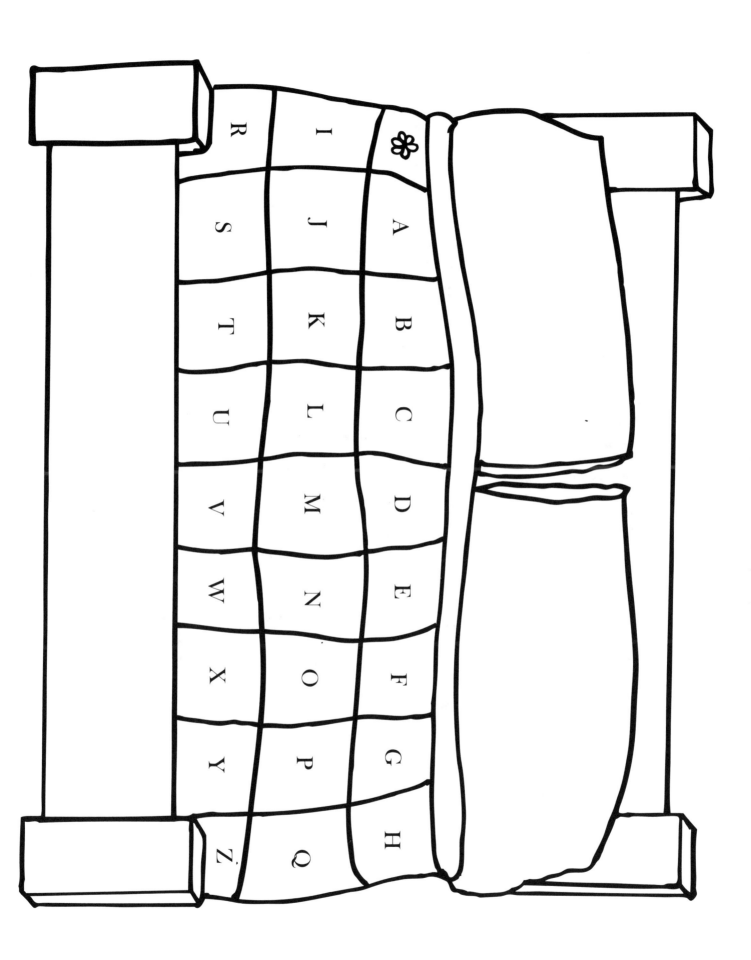

Patchwork Quilt Alphabet Pattern

Q Q Q Q Q Q Q Q Q

Q Q

q q q q q q q q q q q q

q q

Qq Qq Qq Qq Qq

Qq Qq

R — Rain

Introduction

This is a good program to have on hand for a rainy day. A variety of sounds can be incorporated into this program (pitter, patter, tap, tap, tap, drip, drop, etc.). The "r" sound is important to learn on its own before it becomes a blend.

Introductory Poem

It starts with "r" and ends with "ain."
It goes drip, drop on your windowpane.

Finger Play Speller

- Use the finger play glove following the pattern and instructions on pages 13–16.

- Make one each of r, a, i, n for the glove using the patterns on pages 17–18.

- Make one rain finger play character using the pattern on page 172.

- Affix the rain finger play character in the center velcro tab of the glove.

- One by one, attach the r, a, i, n letters onto the glove. Pause between each one, focusing on the sounds and the blends: r ra rai rain. Once "rain" has been achieved, spell the word by pointing to the letters and saying them out loud. You might wish to expand the word to "raindrop" for use in the program.

Name Game

- Have the children think of the name of a person that begins with "r" (Raphael, Randy, Rachel, etc.).

- Have children work on sentences that focus on the "r" sound (Randy rushes rapidly into the rain. Rachel the robin runs 'round and 'round. Etc.). Make the sentences as silly as possible.

Finger Plays

- Make five of the rain finger play characters using the pattern and instructions on page 172.

- Practice rhyming sounds with the

finger plays. Use the ones provided, or look for others. Use the finger play characters to count either up or down with the plays.

Count Down Rhyme

"Five Little Raindrops"

(Sung to the tune "Six Little Ducks.")
Five little raindrops—drip, drip, drop
Hoped the rain would never stop.
But the sun came out and shone away,
And one little raindrop dried up that day.

(Repeat for 4, 3, 2, 1)

Stay and Play Rhyme

"This Little Raindrop"

This little raindrop fell on water.
This little raindrop fell on land.
This little raindrop hit my raincoat.
This little raindrop hit my hand.
And this little raindrop went DRIP, DRIP, DRIP—
Into a puddle grand.

Resources for Storytime

Use some of these books and poems, or any of your favorites, to create a well-rounded storytime program.

Books

Appelt, Kathi. *Rain Dance.* Illustrated by Emilie Chollat. HarperCollins Children's Books, 2001. It's raining, and animals are dancing and counting. One frog hops, two spiders skitter, three chickens flitter …

Arnosky, Jim. *Rabbits and Raindrops.* Penguin Putnam Young Readers, 2001. Rabbit babies are caught in a rainstorm, and other wild animals come to visit.

Bauer, Marion Dane. *Rain.* Illustrated by John Wallace. Aladdin, 2004. Illustrations and simple text explain what rain is; how it is used by plants, birds, and people; and the importance of clean water. A "Ready to Read" book.

Bridges, Margaret Park. *Now What Can I Do?* Illustrated by Melissa Sweet. SeaStar Books, 2001. A little raccoon wonders what to do on a rainy day.

Garelick, May. *Where Does the Butterfly Go When It Rains?* Illustrated by Nicholas Wilson. Mondo Publishing, 2001. A rhythmic text describes what happens to various animals when it rains.

Germein, Katrina. *Big Rain Coming.* Illustrated by Bronwyn Bancroft. Houghton Mifflin, 2000. Residents of an Australian outback anticipate a much-needed rain.

Gorbachev, Valeri. *Nicky and the Rainy Day*. North-South Books, 2002. Nicky comes up with things to do on a rainy day but discovers, when the rain stops, that there are wonders in his own backyard.

Grand, Dee Ann. *My Rainy Day*. Illustrated by Melanie Mitchell. Reader's Digest Children's Books, 2004. A young girl buttons up her raincoat to enjoy a rainy day.

Grubb, Lisa. *Happy Dog!* Penguin Putnam Young Readers, 2003. Jack Cat paints a dog during a rainy Saturday to keep him company.

Harker, Lesley. *Annie's Ark*. Scholastic, 2002. A timeless story retold by Noah's granddaughter, Annie.

Hobbie, Nathaniel. *Priscilla and the Splish-Splash Surprise*. Illustrated by Jocelyn Hobbie. Little, Brown and Company, 2006. Bored after three days of non-stop rain, Priscilla goes outside to perform a rain-stopping dance and meets Posy the Pixie, who teaches her to appreciate both rain and sunshine.

Hull, Maureen. *Rainy Days with Bear*. Illustrated by Leanne Franson. Lobster Press, 2004. When bear suggests taking a trip, the preoccupied writer suggests he imagine going.

Kurtz, Jane. *Rain Romp: Stomping Away a Grouchy Day*. HarperCollins, 2002.

Angry stomps on a rainy day turn to a gleeful "rain romp."

Leonard, Marcia. *Splish, Splash!* Photos by Dorothy Handelman. HarperCollins, 2000. A charming story about getting wet and staying dry on a rainy day.

Manning, Maurie. *The Aunts Go Marching*. Boyds Mills Press, 2003. Dressed in raincoats and carrying umbrellas, a platoon of aunts march through a rainy city in this cumulative rhyme.

McPhail, David. *Big Brown Bear Goes to Town*. Harcourt, 2006. Rat's car fills up with water when it rains, but his friend Big Brown Bear comes to the rescue.

Metzger, Steve. *Rain! Rain! Go Away*. Illustrated by Hans Wilhelm. Scholastic, 2002. When the day turns rainy, the Dinofours discover lots of indoor activities.

Ray, Mary Lyn. *Red Rubber Boot Day*. Illustrated by Lauren Stringer. Voyager Books, 2005. A child describes all the things there are to do on a rainy day.

Root, Phyllis. *Soggy Saturday*. Illustrated by Helen Craig. Candlewick Press, 2001. After a hard rain, the animals on a farm all turn blue.

Schaefer, Lola M. *This Is the Rain*. Illustrated by Jane Wattenberg. Greenwillow Books, 2001. Cumulative text describes how water falls from the clouds and eventually makes its way to the sea.

Scott, Janine. *Rain on the Roof.* Illustrated by Ian Forss. Picture Window Books, 2006. When the farmhouse roof begins to leak, Farmer Claude and Maude seek shelter in the shed with the animals, but when that roof leaks too, they all go to the truck.

Shannon, David. *The Rain Came Down.* Blue Sky Press, 2000. An unexpected shower causes quarreling among community members.

Todd, Barbara. *The Rainmaker.* Art by Rogé. Annick Press, 2003. Clarence discovers a rain tap and meets the Rainmaker.

Yee, Wong Herbert. *Who Likes Rain?* Henry Holt & Company, 2007. A young girl splashing in the rain plays a guessing game with readers about who enjoys a cloudburst.

Poems

"Dapple-Gray" in *Mary Had a Little Jam and Other Silly Rhymes* by Bruce Lansky. Illustrated by Stephen Carpenter. Meadowbrook Creations, 2004.

"Give Yourself to the Rain" in *Give Yourself to the Rain: Poems for the Very Young* by Margaret Wise Brown. Illustrated by Teri L. Weidner. Margaret K. McElderry Books, 2002.

"Michael is Afraid of the Storm" by Gwendolyn Brooks in *A Family of Poems: My Favorite Poetry for Children* compiled by Caroline Kennedy. Illustrated by Jon J. Muth. Hyperion, 2005.

"Rain" by Spike Milligan in *The Usborne Book of Poems for Young Children* compiled by Philip Hawthorn. Illustrated by Cathy Shimmer. Usborne Books, 2004.

"Rain" in *Where the Sidewalk Ends* by Shel Silverstein. HarperCollins 30th Anniversary Ed., 2004.

"Splishy-Sploshy Wet Day" in *Wiggle Waggle Fun: Stories and Rhymes for the Very, Very Young* by Margaret Mayo. Knopf, 2002.

"Spring Rain" in *Seasons: A Book of Poems* by Charlotte Zolotow. Illustrated by Erik Blegvad. HarperTrophy, 2002.

"Windshield Wipers" in *The Llama Who Had No Pajama* by Mary Ann Hoberman. Illustrated by Betty Fraser. Harcourt, 2006.

"Rain on the Housetop" (Traditional)
Rain on the housetop,
Rain on the tree.
Rain on the green grass,
But don't rain on me!

Alphabet Activities

ABC Connect-the-Dots

Copy one pattern on page 173 for each child. Have the children connect the dots from A to Z to find the mystery picture.

ABC Raindrops

Enlarge and copy one each of the patterns on pages 174–175 for each child. Have the children color the cloud and the raindrops and cut out the raindrops. The children can match the alphabet raindrops to the appropriate spot on the cloud page then glue them in place.

Creative Activities

Misty Picture

Give each child a sheet of light blue construction paper. Have them draw an outdoor scene. Mix a small container of grey paint. Dip a toothbrush in the paint. Holding the toothbrush over a child's picture, rub your fingers along the toothbrush bristles to make a spatter effect over the picture. The result is a misty rain on the drawing. Repeat the process with each child's picture.

Umbrellas

This is a good craft to make for a rainy day. Use half of a paper plate for the top and a Popsicle stick or a bent pipe cleaner for the handle. Have the children color their umbrellas.

Rain Sounds

Children can approximate the sound of rain by swirling a few split peas in a metal pie plate.

Gumdrop Snack

"If all of the raindrops were lemon-drops and gumdrops, oh what a rain it would be."

This is a cute song to work into the theme, and gumdrops are always well-received by children.

Creating Rain Characters

Make five raindrops.

- Trace the rain pattern onto gray fun foam.
- Cut out all the pieces.
- Glue on two roly eyes.
- Apply a mouth using black fabric paint.
- Glue velcro to back.

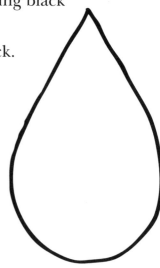

Rain

_ain

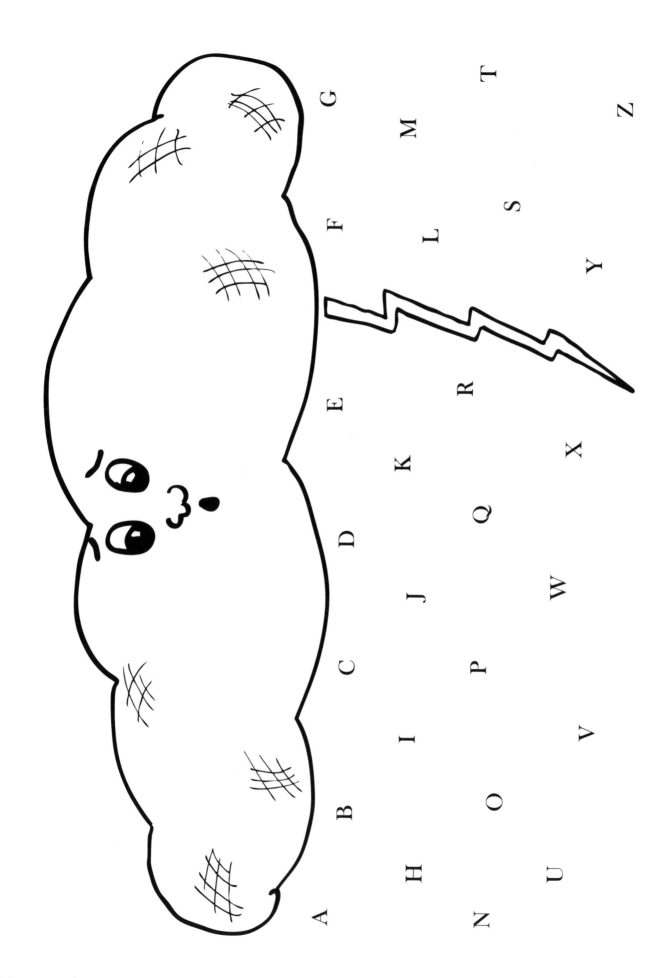

A B C D E F G

H I J K L M

N O P Q R S T

U V W X Y Z

Raindrop Patterns

R R R R R R R R R

R — — — — — — — — — — — — — — — — R

r r r r r r r r r r r r r

r — — — — — — — — — — — — — — — — r

Rr Rr Rr Rr Rr Rr Rr

Rr — — — — — — — — — — — — — — Rr

S – Snake

Introduction

As with insects, children find a fascination with snakes. These slithering creatures are both entertaining and captivating to youngsters. The "sss" sound they make lends itself well to teaching the letter "s" and the sound it makes.

Introductory Poem

He starts with "s" and ends with "nake," and "sss, sss, sss" is the sound he'll make.

Finger Play Speller

- Use the finger play glove following the pattern and instructions on pages 13–16.

- Make one each of: s, n, a, k, e for the glove using the patterns on pages 17–18.

- Make one snake finger play character using the pattern on page 181.

- Affix the snake finger play character in the center velcro tab of the glove.

- One by one, attach the s, n, a, k, e letters onto the glove. Pause between each one, focusing on the sounds and the blends: s sn sna snak snake. Once "snake" has been achieved, spell the word by pointing to the letters and saying them out loud.

Name Game

- Have the children think of the name of a person that begins with "s" (Sammy, Shirley, Steven, etc).

- Have children work on sentences that focus on the "s" sound (Sammy the snake screams when he sees a spider. Shirley snake sports a speckled sunbonnet. Etc.). Make the sentences as silly as possible.

Finger Plays

- Make five of the snake finger play characters using the pattern and instructions on page 181.

- Practice rhyming sounds with finger plays. Use the ones provided, or look for others. Use the finger play characters to count either up or down with the plays.

Count Up Rhyme

"One Snake" (Sung to the tune "She'll Be Coming 'Round the Mountain.")

There was one snake hiding in the grass: ssss ssss.

There was one snake hiding in the grass: ssss ssss.

Oh, he slithered 'round the bend where he met a new snake friend.

And the friend came and joined him at the pass: ssss ssss.

(Repeat for 2, 3, 4)

Count Down Rhyme

"Five Slithery Snakes"

Five slithery snakes, sliding by the door.

One slipped away, and then there were four.

Four slithery snakes, sneaking 'round a tree.

One slipped away, and then there were three.

Three slithery snakes, hissing right at you.

One slipped away, and then there were two.

Two slithery snakes, seeking out some fun.

One slipped away, and then there was one.

One slithery snake, sad without his friends,

Slipped away to find them, and that's how this rhyme ends.

Resources for Storytime

Use some of these books and poems, or any of your favorites to create a well-rounded storytime program.

Books

Aruego, José and Ariane Dewey. *The Last Laugh*. Dial Books for Young Readers, 2006. A wordless tale in which a clever duck outwits a bullying snake.

Banks, Kate. *The Bird, the Monkey and the Snake in the Jungle*. Illustrated by Tomek Bogacki. Farrar, Straus and Giroux, 2003. A rebus story featuring three creatures searching for a new home.

Cannon, Janell. *Verdi*. Harcourt, 2001. Verdi the snake refuses to turn green when he grows and lands himself in a heap of trouble.

Gordon, Sharon. *Guess Who Hisses*. Benchmark Books, 2005. One of the Bookworms "Guess Who" series.

Jonell, Lynne. *I Need a Snake*. Illustrated by Petra Mathers. Putnam, 2000. A young boy who wants a pet snake finds an inventive way to have one.

Law, Felicia. *Rumble Meets Vikki Viper*. Illustrated by Yoon-Mi Pak. Picture Window Books, 2006. While leaders of the orchestra argue about whether the violinist snake can come into the hotel, she slithers in, eats some porridge, and falls asleep in a just-right bed.

Lester, Julius. *Why Heaven is Far Away.* Illustrated by Joe Cepeda. Scholastic, 2002. When people and animals try to climb ladders to Heaven to escape problems with snakes, it is decided that Heaven needs to be farther away.

Noble, Trinka Hakes. *Jimmy's Boa and the Bungee Jump Slam Dunk.* Illustrated by Steven Kellogg. Penguin Putnam Young Readers, 2003. Jimmy's boa constrictor creates havoc in his gym class, and his antics lead to the formation of an unusual basketball team. See other Jimmy's Boa books.

Renaud, Philip Francis. *The Adventures of Sonny the Snow Snake.* Illustrated by Lori Womers. Renaud Co., 2002. An informative story about a rarely seen snake of the north.

San Souci, Daniel. *The Dangerous Snake and Reptile Club.* Tricycle Press, 2004. A group of friends form a club displaying finds from their vacation, including a king snake.

Siegenthaler, Rolf. *Never Fear, Snake My Dear!* North-South Books, 2001. A caged snake dreams about freedom and going back to his homeland, and a mouse helps him out.

Spohn, Kate. *Turtle and Snake's Day at the Beach.* Viking, 2003. Turtle and Snake enter a sand-castle contest, but their castle disappears. See also *Turtle and Snake Go Camping.*

Stroud, Bettye. *Dance Y'all.* Illustrated by Cornelius Van Wright and Ying-Hwa Hu. Marshall Cavendish, 2001. With help from relatives, Jack Henry overcomes his fear of the long coachwhip snake he's seen in the barn.

Welling, Peter J. *Shawn O'Hisser, the Last Snake in Ireland.* Pelican Publishing, 2002. "Are there snakes in Ireland?" Shawn O'Hisser can tell you because he unraveled that mystery many years ago. A new twist to an old tale.

Whitaker, Zai. *Kali and the Rat Snake.* Illustrated by Srividya Natarajan. Kane/Miller Book Publishers, 2006. Kali's father is a snake catcher, but sometimes Kali is embarrassed by this.

Willis, Jeanne. *Be Gentle, Python!* Carolrhoda, 2001. On Python's first day of school, she can't stop squeezing her classmates, until Elephant accidentally shows her how it feels.

Poems

"Boa Constrictor" in *Where the Sidewalk Ends* by Shel Silverstein. HarperCollins, 30th Anniversary Special Ed., 2004.

"Gimme a Sssqueeeze" in *Bear Hugs:*

Romantically Ridiculous Animal Rhymes by Karma Wilson. Illustrated by Suzanne Watts. Margaret K. McElderry Books, 2005.

"I am a Snake" in *Moon, Have You Met My Mother?* by Karla Kuskin. Knopf, 2002.

"Jake, Jake, Garter Snake" in *See Saw Saskatchewan: More Playful Poems from Coast to Coast* by Robert Heidbreder. Illustrated by Scot Ritchie. Kids Can Press, 2003.

"Oh Sleek Bananaconda" in *Scranimals: Poems by Jack Prelutsky*. Jack Prelutsky. Illustrated by Peter Sís. Greenwillow Books, 2002.

"Python Party" in *Python Play and Other Recipes for Fun* by Robert Heidbreder. Stoddart, 1999.

"Seven Snails and Seven Snakes" in *The Frogs Wore Red Suspenders* by Jack Prelutsky. Illustrated by Petra Mathers. Greenwillow Books, 2002.

Alphabet Activities

ABC Connect-the-Dots

Copy the pattern on page 182 for each child. Have the children connect the dots from A to Z to find the mystery picture.

ABC Snake Puzzle

Enlarge and copy one each of the patterns on pages 183–184 for each child. Glue the pages to Bristol board. Have the children color and cut out the pages. The puzzle can be assembled by following the alphabet in order.

Creative Activities

Hanging Snake

Enlarge and copy one pattern on page 181 for each child. Have the children color in the snake. Starting at the outer edge, cut the snake in a spiral pattern, following the dotted line. Punch a hole at the top of the snake head and hang with string.

Play-dough Snake

Give each child a small portion of play-dough. You can either purchase some playdough or use the following recipe to make some. Have the children roll their dough to form a snake. Enlarge the head area by pinching the dough. Add roly eyes if desired. Encourage children to form the letter "s" with the dough.

- DRY (mix in medium pan)
- WET (mix together)
- 1–2 packages Kool Aid (pick a color)
- 2 cups water
- 2 cups flour
- 2 tablespoons cooking oil
- 1 cup salt
- 4 teaspoons cream of tartar

1. Add wet ingredients to dry ingredients.

2. Cook 3–5 minutes over medium heat, stirring constantly.

3. Knead 3–5 minutes.

4. Store in an airtight container until ready to use.

Pasta Snake

String penne pasta together to form a snake. Children may color their snake with markers, or optionally you can prepare the pasta earlier by rolling in green or brown paint. Encourage children or their parents to write letters of the alphabet on each piece of pasta.

Creating Snake Characters

Make five snakes.

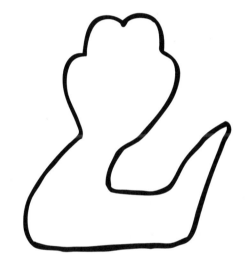

- Trace the snake pattern onto green fun foam.

- Cut out all the pieces.

- Glue on roly eyes and optionally apply a forked tongue with red fabric paint and body patterns with green fabric paint.

- Glue Velcro to back.

Snake

Hanging Snake Pattern

_nake

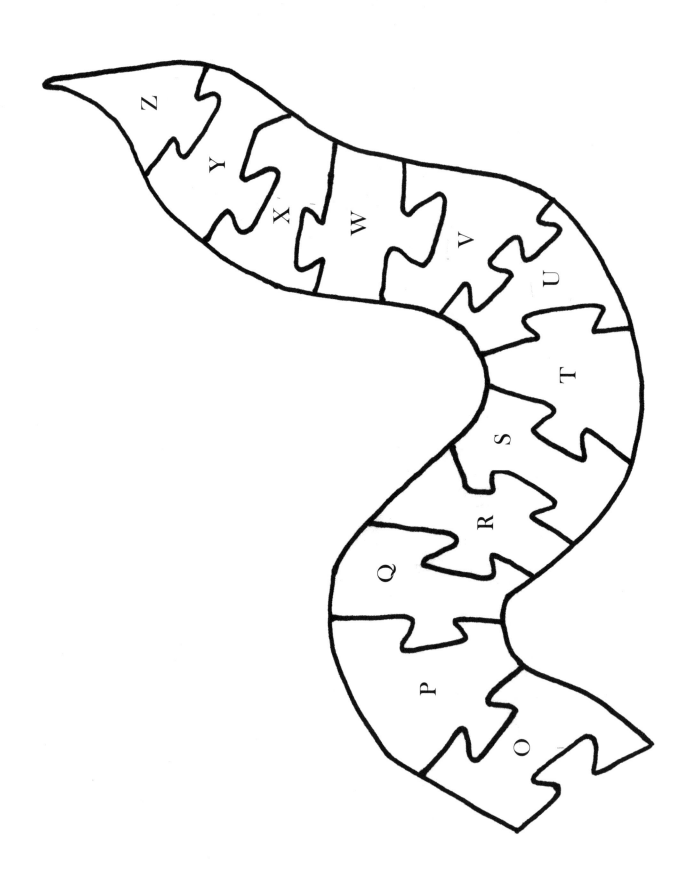

S S S S S S S S S S S S

S - S

S S S S S S S S S S S S S

S - - - - - - - - - - - - - - - - - - - S

Ss Ss Ss Ss Ss Ss Ss

Ss - - - - - - - - - - - - - - - - Ss

T – Train

Introduction

This is a favorite topic with children. Trains can be used as a program on their own, or they can be incorporated into a travel or transportation theme. The "ch, ch" sound of the choo-choo chugging down the track introduces an important blend, while the "t" sound is a crucial letter to understand.

Introductory Poem

It starts with "t" and ends with "rain."
It goes "choo, choo" in sun and rain.

Finger Play Speller

- Use the finger play glove following the pattern and instructions on pages 13–16.

- Make one each of t, r, a, i, n for the glove using the patterns on pages 17–18.

- Make one train finger play character using the pattern on page 190.

- Affix the train finger play character in the center velcro tab of the glove.

- One by one, attach the t, r, a, i, n letters onto the glove. Pause between each one, focusing on the sounds and the blends: t tr tra trai train. Once "train" has been achieved, spell the word by pointing to the letters and saying them out loud.

Name Game

- Have the children think of the name of a person that begins with "t" (Tommy, Tanya, Trent, etc.).

- Have children work on sentences that focus on the "t" sound (Tommy the train traveled the tracks. Tanya is tickled to try the trampoline. Etc.). Make the sentences as silly as possible.

Finger Plays

- Make five of the train finger play character, using the pattern and instructions on page 190.

- Practice rhyming sounds with the finger plays. Use the ones provided, or look for others. Use the finger play characters to count either up or down with the plays.

Count Down Rhyme

"Five Little Trains" (Sung to the tune "Five Little Ducks" in *Eye Winker, Tom Tinker, Chin Chopper: Fifty Musical Fingerplays* by Tom Glazer. Illustrated by Ron Himler. Doubleday, 1973.)

Five little trains on the railroad track

Ran through the town with a clickety-clack.

The engineer called, "Come back, come back!"

But only four little trains came back.

(Repeat for 4, 3, 2, 1)

Count Up Rhyme

"One Little Train"

One little train called, "CHOO CHOO CHOO!"

Along came another, and then there were two.

Two little trains were fast and free.

Along came another, and then there were three.

Three little trains with a load of iron ore.

Along came another, and then there were four.

Four little trains, scheduled to arrive.

Along came another, and then there were five.

"DING DING DONG" went the railway light.

And the five little trains rolled out of sight.

Resources for Storytime

Use some of these books and poems, or any of your favorites, to create a well-rounded storytime program.

Books

Awdry, Reverand W. *Edward the Blue Engine*. Random House, 2003. A favorite with preschoolers; any of the Thomas series is suitable.

Brown, Margaret Wise. *Two Little Trains*. Illustrated by Leo and Diane Dillon. HarperCollins, 2001. Another classic by Brown. Two trains travel on separate tracks until the end of the story when they come together as a real train and a toy train.

Crunk, Tony. *Railroad John and the Red Rock Run*. Illustrated by Michael Austin. Peachtree Publishers, 2006. Lonesome Bob and Granny Apple Fritter rely on Railroad John to get them to Red Rock in time for a wedding.

Drummond, Allan. *Casey Jones*. Farrar, Straus and Giroux, 2001. A saga of the engineer hero told in verse.

Hillenbrand, Will. *Down By the Station*. Harcourt, 2002. Who rides the zoo train early in the morning?

Hooray for Thomas! and Other Thomas the Tank Engine Stories. Random House, 2005. Based on the railway series by the Reverend W. Awdry.

Hubbell, Patricia. *Trains: Steaming! Pulling! Huffing!* Illustrated by Megan Halsey and Sean Addy. Marshall Cavendish, 2005. Rhyming text presents the characteristics of various kinds of trains.

Landolf, Diane Wright. *Sammy's Bumpy Ride*. Random House, 2005. Sammy and the Koala brothers help build a train track. A "Step Into Reading" book.

Lawson, Julie. *Bear on the Train*. Illustrated by Brian Deines. Kids Can Press, 2001. A hungry bear boards a train and promptly falls asleep. See also *Emma and the Silk Train*.

Lewis, Kevin. *Chugga-Chugga Choo-Choo*. Illustrated by Daniel Kirk. Hyperion, 2001. A toy engineer and his son drive a train loaded with toys.

London, Jonathan. *A Train Goes Clickety-Clack*. Illustrated by Denis Roche. Henry Holt & Company, 2007. Rhyming text describes the sounds of, and uses for, different kinds of trains.

Lund, Deb. *All Aboard the Dinotrain*. Illustrated by Howard Fine. Harcourt, 2006. Dinosaurs seeking adventure on a train ride have some unexpected surprises along the way.

Mayo, Margaret. *Choo Choo Clickety-Clack*. Illustrated by Alex Ayliffe. Lerner Publishing Group, 2005. Rhythmic sounds imitate trains, planes, and other busy transports that come and go.

Parker, Marjorie Blain. *Hello Freight Train!* Illustrated by Bob Kolar. Scholastic, 2005. A "Scholastic Reader."

Piper, Watty. *The Little Engine that Could*. Illustrated by Phil A. Smouse. Barbour, 2002. The traditional story of the little engine determined to climb a steep hill to save a stranded train full of toys.

Sobel, June. *The Goodnight Train*. Illustrated by Laura Huliska-Beith. Harcourt, 2006. A child's bedtime ritual follows the imaginary journey of a goodnight train's trip to the dreamland station.

Spanyol, Jessica. *Go Bugs Go!* Candlewick Press, 2006. The adventures and misadventures of the Bugs as they travel in various types of automobiles, airplanes, and trains.

Thomas' Big Storybook. Illustrated by David Mitton, Kenny McArthur, and Terry Permane. Random House Children's Books, 2006. A collection of twenty-four stories based on the Railway series by the Reverend W. Awdry.

Wilcoxen, Chuck. *Niccolini's Song.* Illustrated by Mark Buehner. Puffin, 2006. A gentle night watchman at the railroad yard lulls anxious train engines to sleep by singing just the right song.

Poems

"From a Railway Carriage" by Robert Louis Stevenson in *The Usborne Book of Poems for Young Children* compiled by Philip Hawthorn. Illustrated by Cathy Shimmen. Usborne Books, 2004.

"Puff-Puff, Choo-Choo!" and "Toot-Toot! Train!" in *Wiggle Waggle Fun: Stories and Rhymes for the Very, Very Young* by Margaret Mayo. Knopf, 2002.

"The Train from Lock Brane" by Phillip Hawthorn in *The Usborne Book of Poems for Young Children*. Illustrated by Cathy Shimmen. Usborne Books, 2004.

"I've Been Working on the Railroad"
(traditional)

I've been working on the railroad,
All the live long day.
I've been working on the railroad,
Just to pass the time of day.
Can't you hear the whistle blowing?
Rise up so early in the morn'.
Can't you hear the Captain shouting?
"Dinah, blow your horn."

Alphabet Activities

ABC Connect-the-Dots

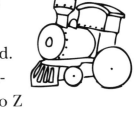

Copy one pattern on page 191 for each child. Have the children connect the dots from A to Z to find the mystery picture.

ABC Train

Enlarge and copy one each of the patterns on pages 192–194 for each child. Have the children color and cut out the trains. The children can assemble their trains in order by following the letters of the alphabet.

Creative Activities

Train Picture

Copy one train picture from page 195 for each child. Have the children color in their train and cut it out. Cut one wheel set pattern onto black bristol board. Fasten the wheels onto the picture with paper fasteners to make moving wheels.

Human Train

Have the children line up and place their hands on the hips of the person in front of them. Play some suitable music and have the children move while making train sounds.

Box Train

An alternative to the above is to line up several large boxes with the tops cut off. Have the children climb in and pretend they are on a train.

Train Craft

Children can make their own trains with a milk carton and some bristol board for wheels. Have the children decorate their trains as they wish.

Train Snack Server

Make the train craft above on a slightly larger scale. Take a second small box and create a boxcar. Fill the boxcar with cookies or other treats and have the children pick out a snack.

Creating Train Characters

Make five trains.

- Trace the train pattern onto red fun foam.
- Trace the wheel patterns onto black fun foam.
- Cut out all the pieces.
- Glue the large wheel to back of train.
- Glue the small wheel to front of train.
- Apply a bar between the two wheels with black fabric paint.
- Apply other details as desired with black fabric paint.
- Glue velcro to back.

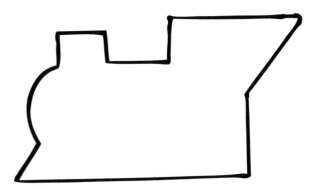

Train

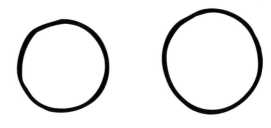

Wheels

_____ rain

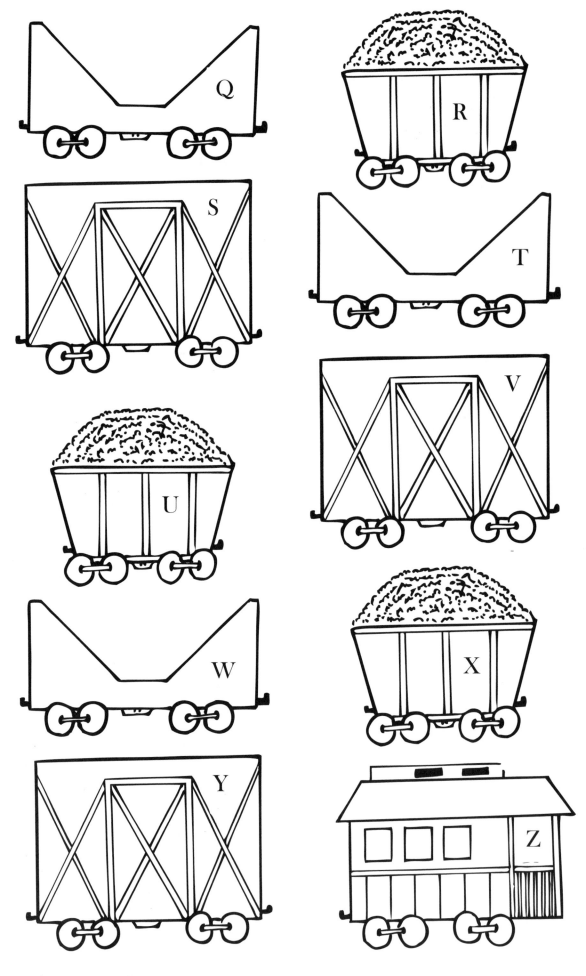

Train Picture

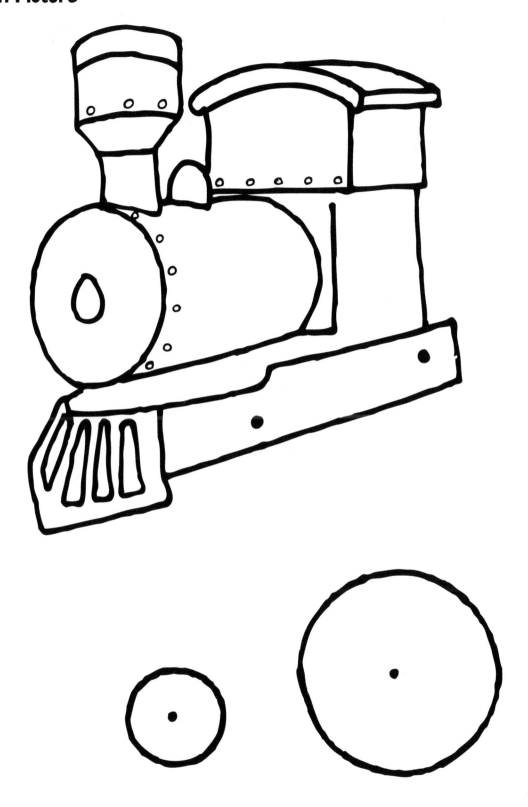

T T T T T T T T T T T T T

T — — — — — — — — — — — — — T

t t t t t t t t t t t t t t t

t — — — — — — — — — — — — — — t

Tt Tt Tt Tt Tt Tt Tt Tt

Tt — — — — — — — — — — — — Tt

U – Urn

Introduction

Finding a word beginning with "u" that could be viewed as a subject and was five letters or less in length was a challenge. This is a suggestion; however you could choose to use a word like "umbrella" or "unicorn," omitting the spelling glove, or spelling on a flannel board or markerboard. The short "u" sound is a necessary sound for children to know.

Introductory Poem

It starts with "u" and ends with "rn." It rhymes with burn, and turn, and churn.

Finger Play Speller

- Use the finger play glove following the pattern and instructions on pages 13–16.
- Make one each of u, r, n for the glove using the patterns on pages 17–18.

- Make one urn finger play character using the pattern on page 200.
- Affix the urn finger play character in the center velcro tab of the glove.
- One by one, attach the u, r, n letters onto the glove. Pause between each one, focusing on the sounds and the blends: u ur urn. Once "urn" has been achieved, spell the word by pointing to the letters and saying them out loud.

Name Game

- Have the children think of the name of a person that begins with "u" (Ursula, Unger, Uxley, etc.).
- Have children work on sentences that focus on the "u" sound (Uxley is under an ugly umbrella. Ursula's urn is upstairs. Etc.). Make the sentences as silly as possible.

Finger Plays

- Make five of the urn finger play characters using the pattern and instructions on page 200.

- Practice rhyming sounds with the finger plays. Use the ones provided, or look for others. Use the finger play characters to count either up or down with the plays.

Count Up Rhyme

"Mary Made a Little Urn" (Sung to the tune "Mary Had a Little Lamb.")
Mary made a little urn.
On the wheel, watch it turn.
Mary made a little urn,
Oh look, she's made another!

Repeat for 2, 3, 4

Count Up Rhyme

"One Little Urn"
One little urn, painted brilliant blue.
A potter made another, and then there were two.

Two little urns, perfect as can be.
A potter made another, and then there were three.

Three little urns, sitting on the floor.
A potter made another, and then there were four.

Four little urns, with colors so alive.
A potter made another, and then there were five.

Resources for Storytime

Use some of these books and poems, or any of your favorites, to create a well-rounded storytime program.

Books

Andrews-Goebel, Nancy. *The Pot that Juan Built*. Pictures by David Diaz. Lee & Low Books, 2002. A cumulative rhyme summarizes the work of renowned Mexican potter, Juan Quezada.

Atkin, Jacqui. *Pottery Basics*. Barron's Ed. Series, 2005. An instructional book that may be good as reference.

Ballard, Carol. *How We Use Soil*. Raintree, 2005. Includes a section on using soil for pottery.

Chanko, Pamela, and Betsey Chessen. *Clay Art with Gloria Elliott*. Scholastic, 1999. Shows how to make simple objects with clay.

Ellis, Mary. *Ceramics for Kids: Creative Clay Projects to Pinch, Roll, Coil, Slam, and Twist*. Sterling Publishing, 2002. An introduction to clay and pottery.

Price, Christine. *Valiant Chatee-Maker: A Folktale of India*. Warne, 1965. A timid pottery maker inadvertently captures a tiger and becomes a hero. The book may be difficult to locate, but it is a worthwhile addition to the topic.

Salzmann, Mary Elizabeth. *The Race for the Vase*. ABDO Publishing, 2005. Rhyming riddles in text.

Scanlon, Elizabeth Garton. *A Sock Is a Pocket for Your Toes: A Pocket Book*. Illustrated by Robin Preiss Glasser. HarperCollins, 2004. A celebration of non-traditional pockets, including a vase as a pocket for a rose.

Weninger, Brigitte. *It Was Me, Mom!* Illustrated by Stephanie Roehe. Translated by Charise Myngheer. Minedition, 2005. After breaking his mother's favorite vase, Miko tries to conceal his involvement but is relieved when his toy animal Mimiki tells Mom the truth.

Poems

"Ode on a Grecian Urn" by George Keats. Check in general poetry books or on the Internet. This is an adult poem, though it is quite rhythmic.

"The Prettiest Urn"

A prettier urn I never once saw.
A prettier one there can't be.
I know for a fact it's the prettiest one.
Because it was crafted by me.

Alphabet Activities

ABC Connect-the-Dots

Copy one pattern on page 201 for each child. Have the children connect the dots from A to Z to find the mystery picture.

ABC Urn "Shelfabet"

Enlarge and copy one each of the patterns on pages 202–203 for each child. Have the children color the shelves and the urns and cut out the urns. The children can match the alphabet urns to the appropriate spot on the shelf then glue them in place.

Creative Activities

Play-dough Urn

Give each child enough play-dough to model a small urn. Encourage children to make different types, shapes, and patterns. Either purchase the play-dough, or follow the recipe in the snake section.

Paper Cup Urn

Give each child one paper cup and two pipe cleaners. Have children make their own urn with pipe cleaner handles. Children can decorate their urns with construction paper scraps or with markers.

Urn Bean Bag Toss

Using a large metal or durable urn, have the children try to toss their beanbags into the urn. Have prizes for everyone.

Urn Cookies

Make several cookies shaped like an urn. Use the pattern for the urn characters, or design your own. Give each child one to decorate with icing.

Creating Urn Characters

Make five urns.

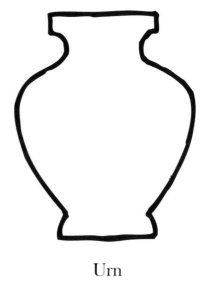

- Trace the urn pattern onto any color of fun foam.

- Cut out all the pieces.

- Shape small pieces of pipe cleaner into handles for the urn.

- Glue handles in place.

- Decorate the urn with various colors of fabric paint.

- Glue velcro to back.

Urn

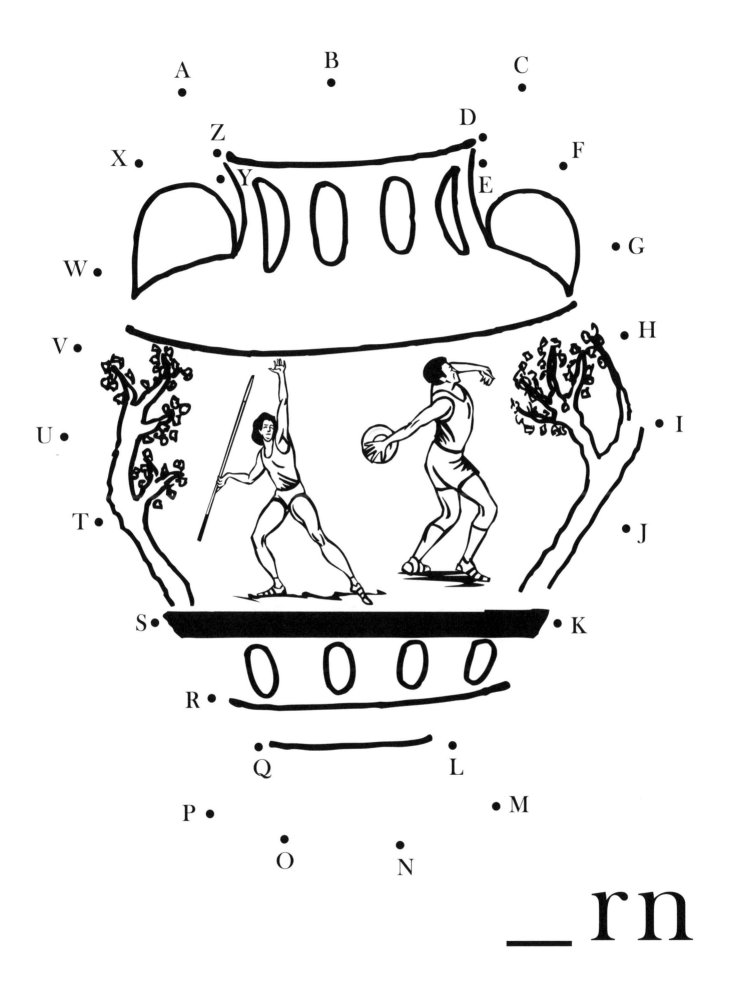

_rn

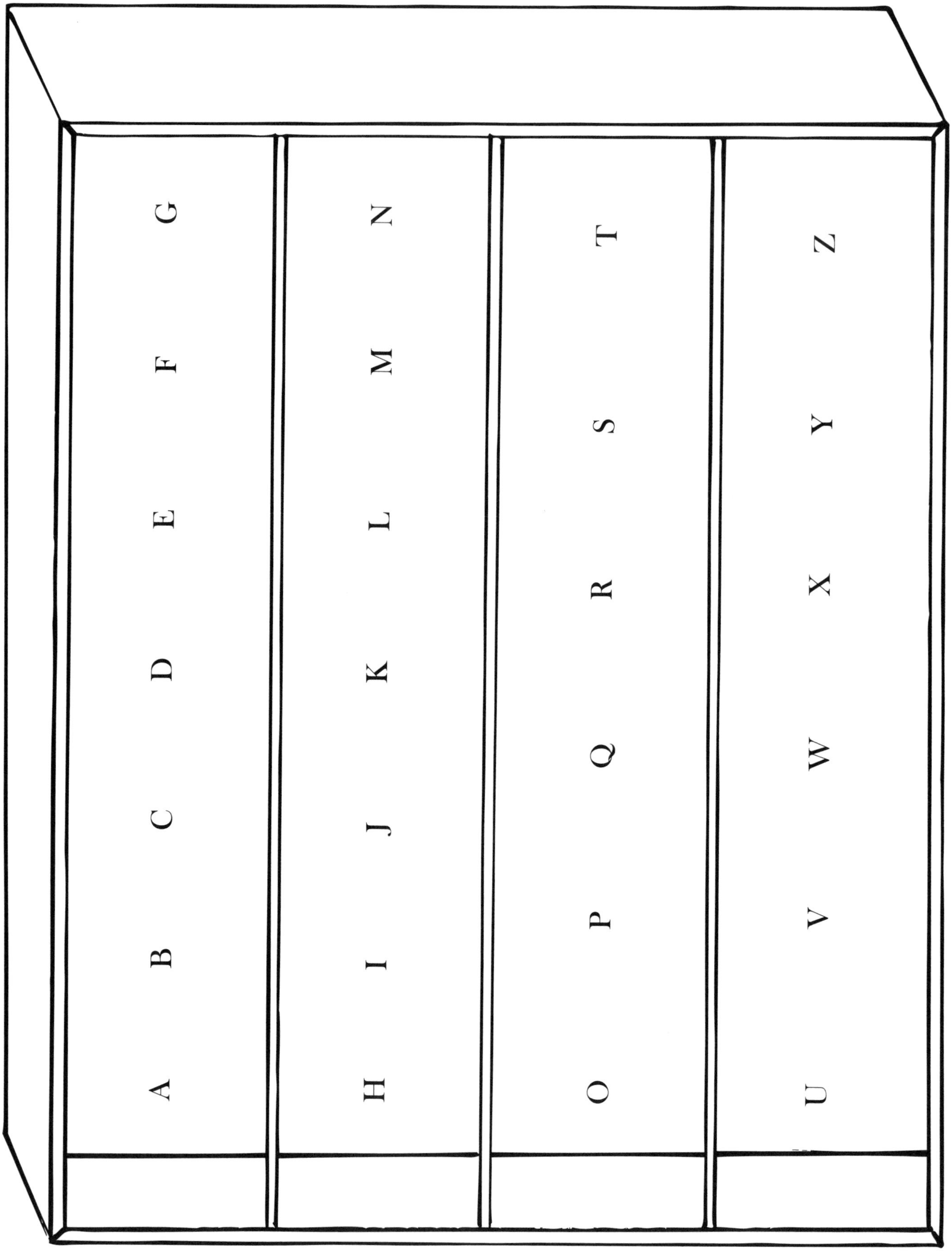
A B C D E F G
H I J K L M N
O P Q R S T
U V W X Y Z

Urn Patterns

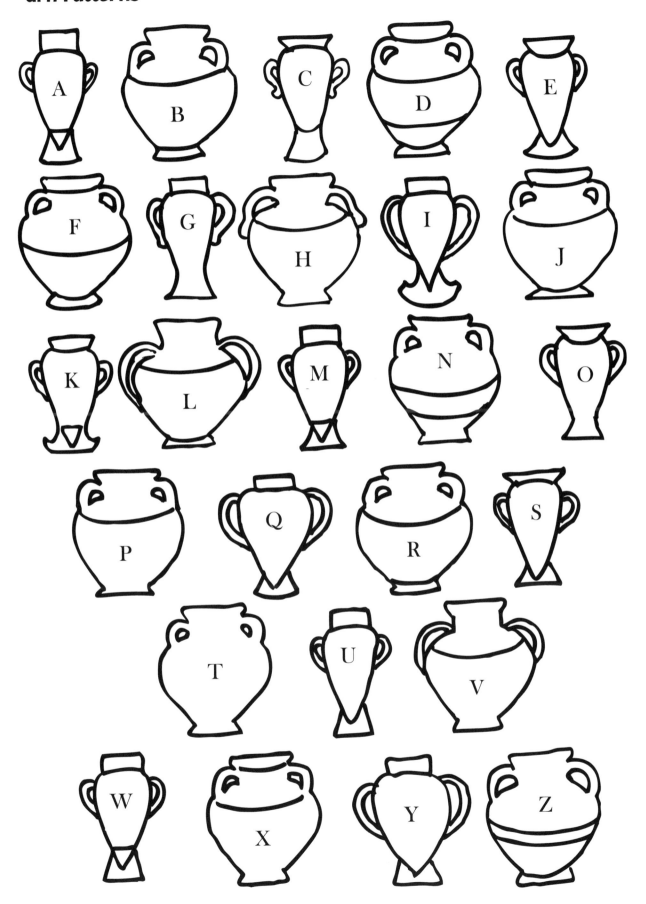

U U U U U U U U U U U U

U U

U U U U U U U U U U U U

U U

Uu Uu Uu Uu Uu Uu

Uu Uu

V – Vine

Introduction

Vines conjure up the image of jungles and swinging monkeys, however vines can also grow in simple home gardens. Jack's mother grew a giant beanstalk in her garden! The sound for "v" is not an easy one to master, so practice is important.

Introductory Poem

It starts with "v" and ends with "ine"
Monkeys swing from this very kind.

Finger Play Speller

- Use the finger play glove following the pattern and instructions on pages 13–16.
- Make one each of v, i, n, e for the glove using the patterns on pages 17–18.
- Make one vine finger play character using the pattern on page 208.
- Affix the vine finger play character in the center velcro tab of the glove.
- One by one, attach the v, i, n, e letters onto the glove. Pause between each one, focusing on the sounds and the blends: v vi vin vine. Once "vine" has been achieved, spell the word by pointing to the letters and saying them out loud.

Name Game

- Have the children think of the name of a person that begins with "v" (Veronica, Victor, Valdez, etc.).
- Have children work on sentences that focus on the "v" sound (Victor vainly vacuums the vines. Veronica eats vines like vegetables. Etc.). Make the sentences as silly as possible.

Finger Plays

- Make five of the vine finger play character using the pattern and instructions on page 208.
- Practice rhyming sounds with the finger plays. Use the ones provided, or look for others. Use the finger play characters to count either up or down with the plays.

Count Down Rhyme

"Five Jungle Vines" (Sung to the tune "Five Little Ducks.")

Five jungle vines in the forest grow.

Waving as monkeys swing to and fro.

One jungle vine breaks—SNAP, SNAP, SNAP!

And only four little vines swing back.

(Repeat for 4, 3, 2, 1)

Count Up Rhyme

"One Little Vine"

One little vine in the jungle grew.

Another one sprouted, and then there were two.

Two little vines, hanging from a tree.

Another one sprouted, and then there were three.

Three little vines touch the jungle floor.

Another one sprouted, and then there were four.

Four little vines, in the jungle thrive.

Another one sprouted, and then there were five.

Resources for Storytime

Use some of these books and poems, or any of your favorites, to create a well-rounded storytime program.

Books (Includes plants and jungles)

Ayres, Katherine. *Up, Down & Around.* Illustrated by Nadine Bernard Westcott. Candlewick Press, 2007. A garden produces a variety of edible plants, such as corn that grows up, onions that grow down, and tomato vines that twine all around.

Carle, Eric. *The Tiny Seed.* Little Simon, 2005. A simple description of a flowering plant's life cycle.

Gage, Wilson. *Mrs. Gaddy and the Fast-growing Vine.* Illustrated by Marylin Hafner. Greenwillow Books, 1985. Mrs. Gaddy buys a fast-growing vine that begins to take over her house, her animals, and herself. An older book, but well worth the effort to find it.

Inches, Allison. *Corduroy's Garden.* Illustrated by Allan Eitzan. Puffin, 2004. Corduroy plants bean seeds for Lisa's garden, but they are both in for a surprise when the beans finally appear on the vines. Based on the bear character by Don Freeman.

Karon, Jan. *The Trellis and the Seed: A Book of Encouragement for All Ages.* Illustrated by Robert Gantt Steele. Puffin, 2005. A small seed surprises itself by becoming a flowering moonflower vine.

Koller, Jackie French. *Seven Spunky Monkeys.* Illustrated by Lynn Munsinger.

Harcourt, 2005. One by one, seven monkeys wind up falling in love. See also *One Monkey Too Many.*

Levert, Mireille. *Lucy's Secret.* Douglas & McIntyre, 2004. Aunt Zinnia and Lucy spend their days in a beautiful garden, but Lucy wants to know how the plants came to be.

Metzger, Steve. *My Seeds Won't Grow!* Illustrated by Hans Wilhem. Scholastic, 2000. Upset that the plants he is growing are the smallest in the class, four-year-old dinosaur Brendon switches his name to another container but then regrets what he has done.

Milgrim, David. *Swing Otto, Swing.* Aladdin, 2005. When Otto the robot has trouble learning to swing on vines like his monkey friends, he decides to make his own swing set instead.

Nolen, Jerdine. *Plantzilla.* Illustrated by David Catrow. Voyager Books, 2002. A boy, his parents, and a science teacher chart the progress of a very unusual plant.

Notkin, Lenore. *The Magic School Bus Gets Planted.* Scholastic, 1997. (Video, 2001.) When the vine that Phoebe is growing isn't as big as she would like, Ms. Frizzle teaches her about how plants eat and grow.

Osborne, Mary Pope. *Kate and the Beanstalk.* Illustrated by Giselle Potter.

Aladdin, 2005. Similar to the original story, a girl climbs to the top of a giant beanstalk and outwits a giant.

Pilkey, Dav. *When Cats Dream.* Scholastic, 1996. When cats dream they can do anything they want, from combing their hair with the moon, to swinging from vines in the jungle.

Poole, Amy Lowry. *The Pea Blossom.* Holiday House, 2005. Based on a Hans Christian Andersen story. In a garden near Beijing five peas in a shell grow and wait to discover what fate has in store for them.

Rey, H. A. *Curious George.* Houghton Mifflin, 2005. The man with the yellow hat finds Curious George in the jungle.

Poems

"My Nose Garden" in *Falling Up* by Shel Silverstein. HarperCollins, 1996.

"Peter Pitcher Planter" in *See Saw Saskatchewan: More Playful Poems from Coast to Coast* by Robert Heidbreder. Illustrated by Scot Ritchie. Kids Can Press, 2003.

"A Very Vigorous Vine"
A very vigorous vine
To another tried to entwine.
Said the one to the other,
"I'll go call our mother,
And she will say it's bedtime."

Alphabet Activities

ABC Connect-the-Dots

Copy one pattern on page 209 for each child. Have the children connect the dots from A to Z to find the mystery picture.

Alphabet Vine

Enlarge and copy one each of the pattern on page 210 for each child. Have the children color and cut out the leaves. Give each child a length of green yarn or string. The children can tape the leaves to the vine in alphabetical order.

Creative Activities

Fingerprint Vine

Make a large classroom mural of a vine stalk. Using green finger paint, have the children create leaves on the vine.

Planting Seeds

Have children plant bean or morning glory seeds in styrofoam cups. As the plants grow, measure the length of the vines.

Tangled Vine

Have the children form a circle. Then, ask them to put their hands inside the circle. Randomly have children grab any hands they see. Once all hands are joined, the children must try to untangle themselves without letting go of any hands.

Wallpaper Vines

Purchase a roll of wallpaper border that features a vine motif. Have the children cut out the vines and arrange them on pieces of paper or a mural.

Creating Vine Characters

Make five vines.

- Trace the leaf pattern onto green fun foam. Make three leaves for each vine (total 15).
- Cut out all the pieces.
- For each vine, glue three leaves to a short piece of green yarn or string.
- Optionally, apply leaf details with green fabric paint.
- Glue velcro to the back of the top leaf.

Leaf

_ine

Vine Pattern

V V V V V V V V V V V

V - V

V V V V V V V V V V V

V - V

Vv Vv Vv Vv Vv Vv

Vv - - - - - - - - - - - - - - - - - Vv

W — Whale

Introduction

Next to dinosaurs, whales are perhaps one of the most fascinating creatures for children. The splashing and spouting of whales lend themselves to sound practice, and the "w" sound can be whispered throughout the program.

Introductory Poem

He starts with "w" and ends with "ale." He splashes in oceans with his tail.

Finger Play Speller

- Use the finger play glove following the pattern and instructions on pages 13–16.

- Make one each of w, h, a, l, e for the glove using the patterns on pages 17–18.

- Make one whale finger play character using the pattern on page 215.

- Affix the whale finger play character in the center velcro tab of the glove.

- One by one, attach the w, h, a, l, e letters onto the glove. Pause between each one, focusing on the sounds and the blends: w wh wha whal whale. Once "whale" has been achieved, spell the word by pointing to the letters and saying them out loud.

Name Game

- Have the children think of the name of a person that begins with "w" (William, Wendy, Wanda, etc.).

- Have children work on sentences that focus on the "w" sound (Wanda and Wendy are wild about whales. Willie the whale wades in the water. Etc.). Make the sentences as silly as possible.

Finger Plays

- Make five of the whale finger play characters using the pattern and instructions on page 215.

- Practice rhyming sounds with the finger plays. Use the ones provided, or look for others. Use the finger play characters to count either up or down with the plays.

Count Up Rhyme

"One Whale Swimming" (Sung to the tune "She'll be Coming 'Round the Mountain.")

There was one whale swimming in the sea: SPLASH, SPLASH!

There was one whale swimming in the sea: SPLASH, SPLASH!

Oh he swam around the bend where he found a new whale friend.

And the whale came and joined him happily: SPLASH, SPLASH!

Count Up Rhyme

"One Little Whale"

One little whale, in the ocean blue,
Swam for a friend—then there were two.

Two little whales, heading out to sea,
Swam for a friend—then there were three.

Three little whales, near the ocean shore,
Swam for a friend—then there were four.

Four little whales, learning how to dive,
Swam for a friend—then there were five.

Resources for Storytime

Use some of these books and poems, or any of your favorites, to create a well-rounded storytime program.

Books

Bunting, Eve. *Whales Passing*. Illustrated by Lambert Davis. Blue Sky Press, 2003. While walking the beach with his father, a young boy imagines what whales would talk about.

Donaldson, Julia. *The Snail and the Whale*. Illustrated by Axel Scheffler. MacMillan Children's Books, 2006. A little snail who hitches a lift on the tail of a whale comes to the rescue of the whale.

London, Jonathan. *Baby Whale's Journey*. Illustrated by Jon Van Zyle. Chronicle Books, 2006. Text and illustrations tell the story of a baby sperm whale's life.

Lucas, David. *Whale*. Andersen, 2006. When a giant whale washes up on shore, no one knows what to do. But with impressive teamwork, a solution is reached.

Man-Kong, Mary. *Theodore and the Whale*. Illustrated by Bernat Serrat. Random House, 1999. From the Theodore Tugboat series. Theodore finds a baby whale and, with the help of other boats, returns him to his pod.

McFarlane, Sheryl. *Waiting for the Whales*. Illustrated by Ron Lightburn.

Orca Book Publishing, 2002. A touching story about the relationship between a grandfather, a granddaughter, and a group of whales that return year after year.

Page, Josephine. *Clifford Saves the Whales*. Illustrated by Carolyn Bracken and Jim Durk. Scholastic, 2002. Clifford wants to go whale watching with friends, but they are afraid he'll scare the whales away. A Scholastic Easy-Reader.

Pfister, Marcus. *Rainbow Fish and the Big Blue Whale*. Translated by J. Alison James. North-South Books, 2001. Rainbow Fish and his friends must share their food and space with a whale that comes to their reef.

Pinkney, Andrea Davis. *Peggony-Po: A Whale of a Tale*. Illustrated by Brian Pinkney. Hyperion Books for Children, 2006. Peggony-Po is determined to catch the huge whale that injured his father.

Rylant, Cynthia. *The Whale*. Simon and Schuster, 2004. When a lonely baby beluga loses his mama, the Lighthouse family helps to bring the two together again.

Schuch, Steve. *Symphony of Whales*. Illustrated by Peter Sylvada. Harcourt, 2002. A girl who communicates with a whale discovers thousands of whales trapped in an inlet.

Steig, William. *Amos & Boris*. Farrar, Straus and Giroux, 2001. A simple, funny story about an unlikely friendship between a mouse and a whale.

Turnbull, Stephen, and Christine Reevey. *The Adventures Aboard the Fundy Starr: a Whale Watching Adventure*. Illustrated by Kory McCumber and Wilfred Morris. Marine Educational Resources, 2000. Captain Bob and his niece and nephew learn about the Bay of Fundy during a whale watching adventure.

Van Dusen, Chris. *Down to the Sea with Mr. Magee*. Chronicle Books, 2006. Mr. Magee and his dog find themselves in a bind that only a pod of whales can save them from.

Young, Selina. *Big Dog and Little Dog Go Sailing*. Crabtree Publishing Company, 2002. Big Dog and Little Dog's adventures on their new boat include fishing, water skiing, and exploring a very unusual island.

Poems

"Melinda Mae" in *Where the Sidewalk Ends* by Shel Silverstein. HarperCollins 30th Anniv. Special Ed., 2004.

"A Thought" and "Whale" in *The Llama Who Had No Pajama: 100 Favorite Poems* by Mary Ann Hoberman. Illustrated by Betty Fraser. Harcourt, 2006.

Alphabet Activities

ABC Connect-the-Dots

Copy one pattern on page 216 for each child. Have the children connect the dots from A to Z to find the mystery picture.

Whale Spout Alphabet

Enlarge and copy one each of the patterns on pages 217–218 for each child. Have the children color the whale and the water drops and cut out the water drops. The children can match the alphabet water drops to the appropriate spot on the whale spout then glue them in place.

Creative Activities

Deep Sea Collage

Have each child design and cut out his or her own whales. Have children glue blue tissue paper to a piece of construction paper to create an ocean background. Add the whales, fish, and a few clouds, and you have a lovely collage.

Whale Mobile

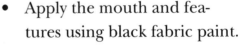

Make two copies of page 219 for each child. Have the children color and cut out the whale patterns. Tie two straws together to form an "X." Fasten whales to pieces of string, and attach other end of string to the straws.

Whale Songs

Try to find a recording of the sounds of humpback whales. Have the children listen to the sounds and then discuss what the sounds might mean.

Whale Dance

While playing classical music, have the children pretend that they are whales. They can pretend to glide in the ocean, splash and dive, and spout water.

How Many Kinds of Whales?

With books or charts, introduce children to the different types of whales. Which whale is the funniest? The largest? The prettiest?

Creating Whale Characters

Make five whales.

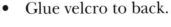

- Trace the whale pattern onto gray fun foam.
- Cut out all the pieces.
- Glue on a small roly eye.
- Apply the mouth and features using black fabric paint.
- Glue velcro to back.

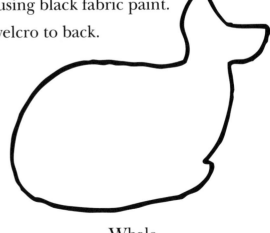

Whale

_hale

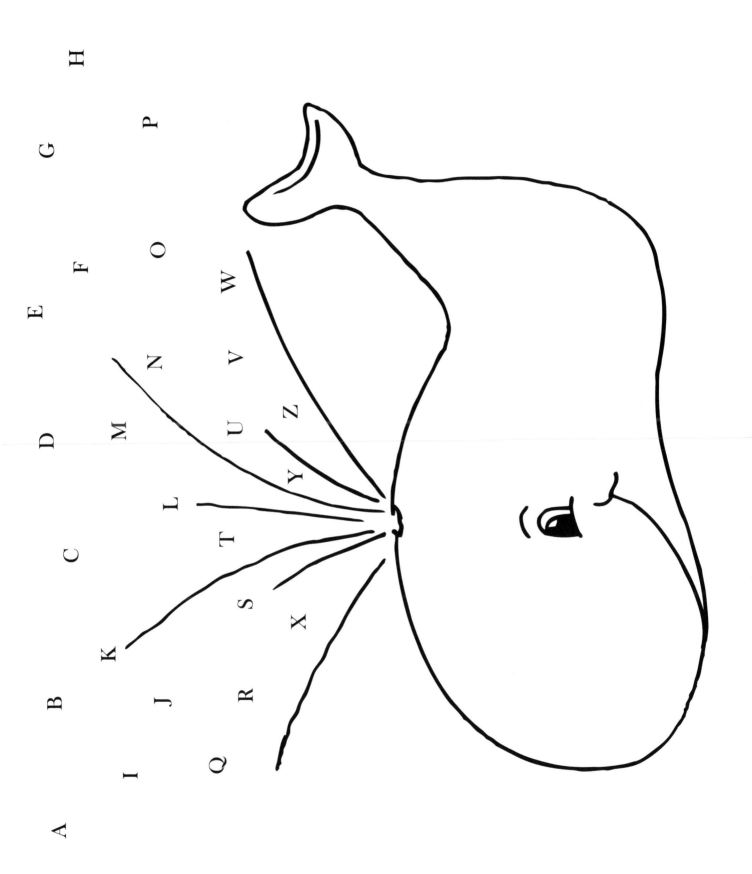

A B C D E F G H I J K L M N O P Q R S T U V W X Y Z

Water Drop Patterns

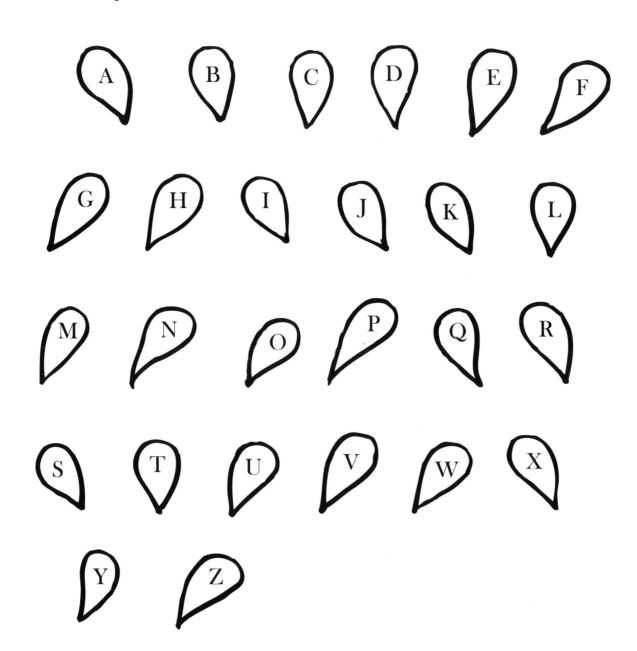

Whale Mobile Patterns

W W W W W W W W

W — — — — — — — — — W

W W W W W W W W W W

W — — — — — — — — W

Ww Ww Ww Ww

Ww — — — — — — — Ww

X — X-ray

Introduction

Children are fascinated by x-rays, though I'm sure their parents are hoping they'll never have the need for one! Although few words begin with "x," the sound is necessary to master for the many words beginning in "e-x."

Introductory Poem

It starts with "x" and ends with "ray." Doctors see them every day.

Finger Play Speller

- Use the finger play glove following the pattern and instructions on pages 13–16.

- Make one each of x, r, a, y for the glove using the patterns on pages 17–18. Optionally, you may choose to use a dash (-) between "x" and "r".

- Make one x-ray finger play character using the pattern on page 224.

- Affix the x-ray finger play character in the center velcro tab of the glove.

- One by one, attach the x, r, a, y letters onto the glove. Pause between each one, focusing on the sounds and the blends: x x-r x-ra x-ray. Once "x-ray" has been achieved, spell the word by pointing to the letters and saying them out loud.

Name Game

- Have the children think of the name of a person that begins with "x" (Xavier, Xanthan, etc.).

- Have children work on sentences that focus on the "x" or the "ex" sound (Xavier expertly examines x-rays. Xanthan exercises on a xylophone. Etc.). Make the sentences as silly as possible.

Finger Plays

- Make five of the x-ray finger play characters using the pattern and instructions on page 224.

- Practice rhyming sounds with the finger plays. Use the ones provided, or look for others. Use the finger play characters to count either up or down with the plays.

Count Up Rhyme

"One X-ray" (Sung to the tune "Pop Goes the Weasel.")

One x-ray upon the wall,

Near the camera shutter.

"Make one more," the doctors roar.

CLICK—there's another!

Repeat for 2, 3, 4

Count Down Rhyme

"Five Little X-rays"

Five little x-rays on the surgeon's door.

A doctor reached for one—then there were four.

Four little x-rays, left for all to see.

A doctor took another—then there were three.

Three little x-rays, black with gray parts too.

A doctor took another—then there were two.

Two little x-rays, the work is nearly done.

A doctor took another—then there was one.

One little x-ray, early in the dawn.

A doctor reached for it—now they're all gone.

Resources for Storytime

Use some of these books and poems, or any of your favorites, to create a well-rounded storytime program.

Books

Ballard, Carol. *Bones*. Heinemann Library, 2003. A factual book about bones.

Cousins, Lucy. *Maisy Goes to the Hospital.* Candlewick Press, 2007. When Maisy bounces a little too high on her trampoline, she falls and hurts her leg. Maisy's friend Charley goes with her to the hospital, where X-rays, a cast, and an overnight stay ensue.

Cuyler, Margery. *Skeleton Hiccups.* Illustrated by S. D. Schindler. Alladin, 2005. A ghost tries to help a skeleton with hiccups.

Johnston, Marianne. *Let's Talk About Going to the Hospital.* PowerKids Press, 1997. Explains what a hospital is, what happens there, and when a patient can go home.

The Magic School Bus: Super Sports Fun. Scholastic, 2004. Ms. Frizzle and her class use sports to solve scientific mysteries. Includes a section on x-rays. (Video/DVD)

McClafferty, Carla Killough. *The Head Bone's Connected to the Neck Bone: The*

Weird, Wacky and Wonderful X-ray. Farrar, Straus and Giroux, 2001. Good for preparation work in describing facts to children.

Weitzman, Elizabeth. *Let's Talk About Having a Broken Bone.* PowerKids Press, 1997. Describes what happens when you break a bone, and how this kind of injury is treated.

Zonta, Pat. *Jessica's X-ray.* Illustrated by Clive Dobson. Firefly, 2006. Illustrations and x-ray images on mylar describe the process.

Poems
"Lonely X-ray"

An x-ray sat upon the wall,
Behind the camera shutter.
He wasn't lonely very long,
Before there was another.

"Bones, Bones"

There are bones in my hands.
There are bones in my feet.
There's a skull in my head.
There's a tailbone on my seat.
These bones can all be x-rayed.
And you can see them all.
You look for broken bones.
If you should have a fall.

Alphabet Activities
ABC Connect-the-Dots

Copy one pattern on page 225 for each child. Have the children connect the dots from A to Z to find the mystery picture.

X-ray Alphabet

Enlarge and copy one each of the patterns on pages 226–227 for each child. Copy the picture of the child holding up the x-ray on gray paper. Have the children color the child's arms and waist, and cut out the bones on the other page. The children can match the alphabet bones to the appropriate spot on the x-ray then glue them in place.

Creative Activities
Pin the Skull on the X-ray

Using a gray piece of bristol board, draw the chest and arms of a skeleton. With a white piece of construction paper, draw and cut out a skull. Similar to "pin the tail on the donkey" have the children try to match the skull to the appropriate place on the skeleton.

Studying X-rays

If a hospital is nearby, determine if any old x-ray images are available for classroom use. Children can examine the x-rays and determine what part of the body they represent.

X-ray Machine

Make a pretend x-ray machine for the classroom using a large box with an opening. In the opening draw an x-ray picture. Have children stand behind the machine and pretend to take pictures.

X-ray Puppet

Make a small hand puppet for each child from felt or construction paper. Have the children draw bones on the puppet using fabric paint or markers.

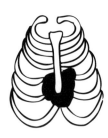

X-ray

Creating X-ray Characters

Make five x-rays.

- Trace the x-ray pattern onto gray fun foam.
- Cut out all the pieces.
- Apply the skeleton using white fabric paint.
- Glue velcro to back.

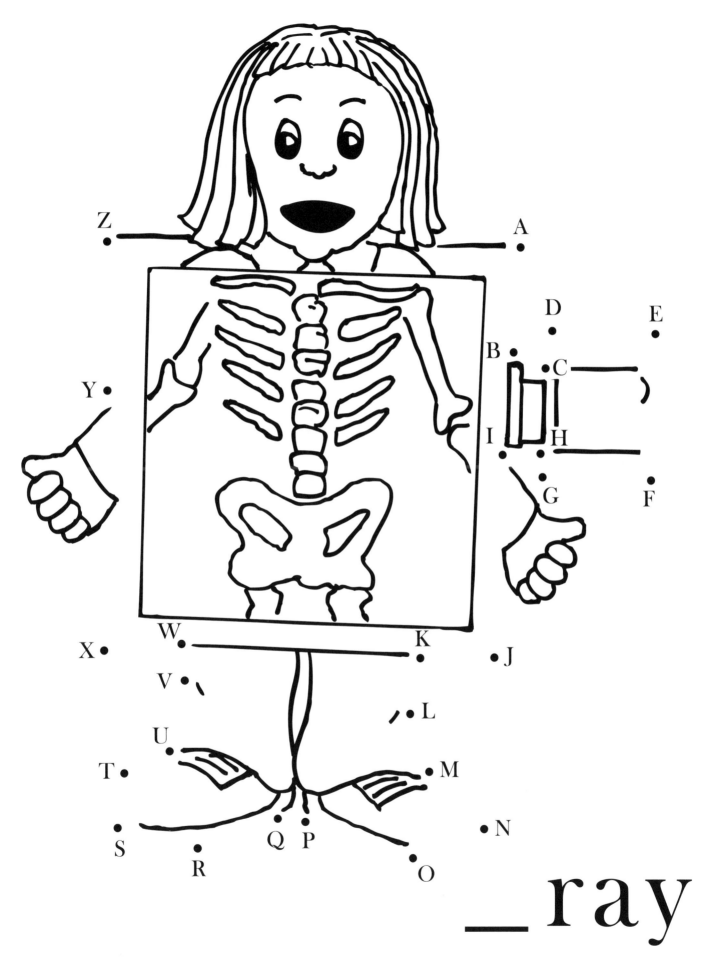

_ray

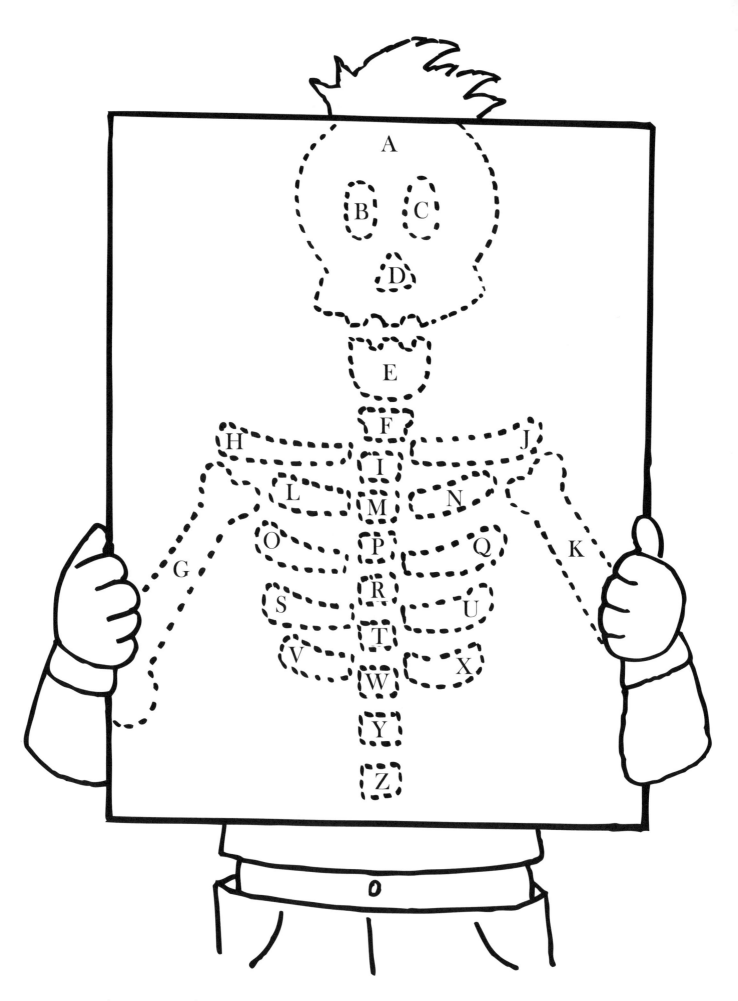

Bone Patterns

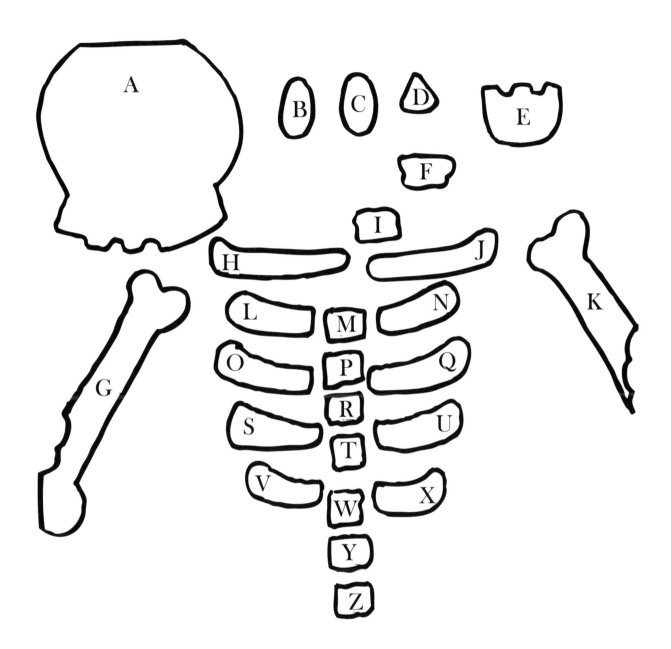

X X X X X X X X X X X

X   X

X X X X X X X X X X X X

X   X

Xx Xx Xx Xx Xx Xx

Xx   Xx

y – Yarn

Introduction

Warm sweaters and cozy mittens introduce children to yarn at an early age. The "y" sound is important to remember at the beginning of a word as well as at the end, as they differ.

Introductory Poem

It starts with "y" and ends with "arn."
It's used to knit, crochet, and darn.

Finger Play Speller

- Use the finger play glove following the pattern and instructions on pages 13–16.

- Make one each of y, a, r, n for the glove using the patterns on pages 17–18.

- Make one yarn finger play character using the pattern on page 232.

- Affix the yarn finger play character in the center velcro tab of the glove.

- One by one, attach the y, a, r, n letters onto the glove. Pause between each one, focusing on the sounds

and the blends: y ya yar yarn. Once "yarn" has been achieved, spell the word by pointing to the letters and saying them out loud.

Name Game

- Have the children think of the name of a person that begins with "y" (Yin, Yogi, Young, etc.).

- Have children work on sentences that focus on the "y" sound (Yin yearns for yellow yarn. Yogi yelps and yodels in York. Etc.). Make the sentences as silly as possible.

Finger Plays

- Make five of the yarn finger play characters using the patterns and instructions on page 232.

- Practice rhyming sounds with the finger plays. Use the ones provided, or look for others. Use the finger play characters to count either up or down with the plays.

Count Down Rhyme

"Knit, Knit, Knit" (Sung to the tune "Row, Row, Row Your Boat.")

Knit, knit, knit a scarf.

With five balls of yarn.

Knit and purl, yarn over, swirl.

Oops! One ball is gone!

Repeat for 4, 3, 2, 1

Count Down Rhyme

"Five Balls of Yarn"

Five balls of yarn, rolling on the floor.

Kitty cat took one, and that left four.

Four balls of yarn, round as round can be.

Kitty cat took one, and that left three.

Three balls of yarn, yellow, red, and blue.

Kitty cat took one, and that left two.

Two balls of yarn, rolled and freshly spun.

Kitty cat took one, and that left one.

One ball of yarn, hiding from the cat.

Kitty cat found it—imagine that!

Resources for Storytime

Use some of these books and poems, or any of your favorites, to create a well-rounded storytime program.

Books

Arrigan, Mary. *Pa Jinglebob and the Grabble Gang.* Illustrated by Korky Paul. Crabtree Publishing Company, 2006. Although Pa Jinglebob wants to knit, he must take action as sheriff of Buckaroo.

Castañeda, Omar S. *Abuela's Weave.* Illustrated by Enrique O. Sanchez. Lee & Low Books, 2002. A young Guatemalan girl and her grandmother grow closer as they weave some special creations in the hopes of selling them.

DeBeer, Hans. *Oh No, Ono!* North-South Books, 2006. Ono the piglet's curiosity results in many mishaps, including being trapped in a ball of yarn while playing with a kitten.

Greenstein, Elaine. *One Little Lamb.* Viking, 2004. Describes how a lamb's coat is made into yarn, which is made into mittens worn by a little girl when she visits the lamb on the farm.

Kent, Jack. *Socks for Supper.* Gareth Stevens, 1993. When a poor couple exchange knitted socks for cheese and milk, they receive more than expected.

Klise, Kate. *Shall I Knit you a Hat?* Illustrated by M. Sarah Klise. Henry

Holt & Company, 2004. When Mother Rabbit knits a hat for Little Rabbit, he suggests they make hats for all of their friends for Christmas.

Lunn, Janet. *Amos's Sweater.* Illustrated by Kim LaFave. Groundwood, 2007. A stubborn sheep doesn't want to part with his wool for making yarn.

Nelson, Robin. *From Sheep to Sweater.* Lerner Publishing Group, 2003. Describes how a sheep grows wool, and how it is processed, spun into yarn and knitted into a sweater.

Oxlade, Chris. *How We Use Wool.* Raintree, 2004. Discusses wool yarn, wool fabrics, knitting, and weaving.

Shannon, Margaret. *The Red Wolf.* Houghton Mifflin, 2002. Roselupin, a princess locked in a tower by her over-protective father, uses yarn to knit a red wolf suit to free herself.

Sloat, Teri. *Farmer Brown Shears His Sheep: A Yarn about Wool.* Illustrated by Nadine Bernard Westcott. DK Publishing, 2000. Farmer Brown shears his sheep and makes the wool into yarn, but after they beg to have it back, he knits the yarn into sweaters for them.

Winthrop, Elizabeth. *The First Christmas Stocking.* Illustrated by Bagram Ibatouline. Random House, 2006. Grieving for her dead mother, a poor girl finds all her dreams fulfilled when, on Christmas Eve, she hangs above her hearth a stocking she has knitted.

Poems

"A Hole in My Sock" in *A Hole in My Sock: A Collection of Poems* by Peter Charles Stainton. Published by Author, 2001.

"Knitted Mittens"

Red yarn, green yarn, yellow, blue—
Any type of yarn will do.
Knit one mitten, work with care.
Knit another, there's a pair.

Alphabet Activities

ABC Connect-the-Dots

Copy one pattern on page 233 for each child. Have the children connect the dots from A to Z to find the mystery picture.

Kitty Cat and Yarn Alphabet

Enlarge and copy one each of the patterns on pages 234–235 for each child. Have the children color the cat and the balls of yarn and cut out the balls of yarn. The children can match the alphabet balls of yarn to the appropriate spot on the cat picture then glue them in place.

Creative Activities

Hot Ball of Yarn

As in the game "hot potato," have the children form a circle. With music playing in the background, children pass the ball of yarn from one person to another. When the music stops, the person holding the ball of yarn is out of the circle. Have a bookmark or special treat ready for each child who is "out."

Papier Maché with Yarn

Using equal amount of water and glue, make a large bowl of paste. Give each child a balloon. Have the children dip strips of yarn in the paste and attach the strips to their balloons. Let the yarn dry and then pop the balloons.

Winding Yarn

Teach the children how to wind balls of yarn. This is good practice for dexterity, rhythm, and patience!

Yarn Pencil Holder

Have children cover frozen juice cans with strips of yarn. This makes a decorative pencil holder.

Creating Yarn Characters

Make five balls of yarn.

- Trace the ball pattern onto various colors of fun foam.
- Cut out all the pieces.
- Glue strips of yarn onto each ball. Use a different color of yarn for each ball, corresponding to the colors of the fun foam.
- Glue velcro to back.

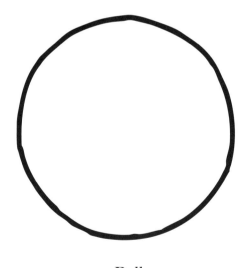

Ball

_ arn

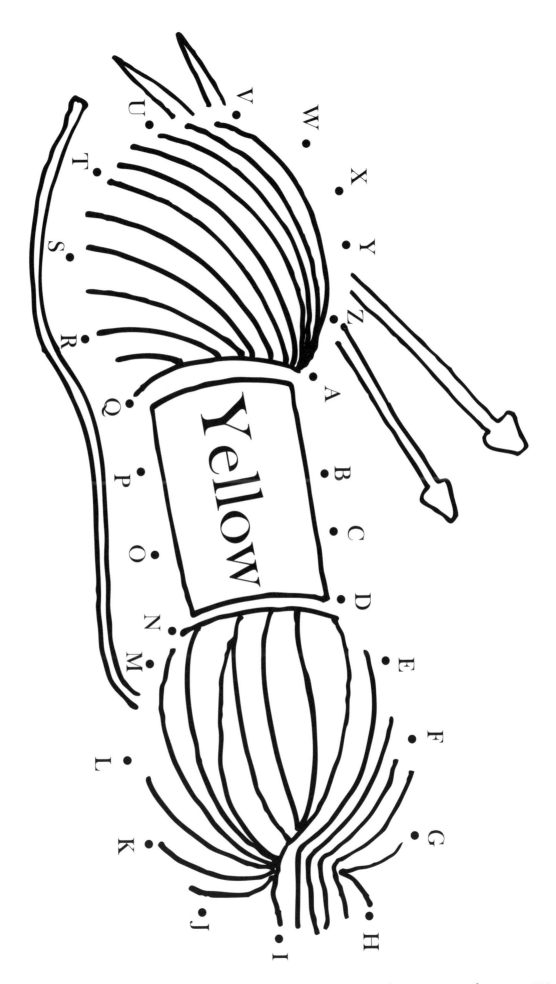

Yellow

A

B

G

H

C

D

I

J

E

M

N

O

P

Q

K

F

L

T

U

V

W

R

Y

Z

X

S

Yarn Patterns

Y Y Y Y Y Y Y Y Y Y Y

Y   Y

Y Y Y Y Y Y Y Y Y Y Y

Y   Y

Yy Yy Yy Yy Yy Yy

Yy   Yy

Z – Zebra

Introduction

Finish off the alphabet with an animal that intrigues children. Is it black with white stripes, or white with black stripes? The "z" sound wraps up the letters in a fun way.

Introductory Poem

She starts with "ze" and ends with "bra." She's stripey-striped from tail to jaw.

Finger Play Speller

- Use the finger play glove following the pattern and instructions on pages 13–16.

- Make one each of z, e, b, r, a for the glove using the patterns on pages 17–18.

- Make one zebra finger play character using the pattern on page 240.

- Affix the zebra finger play character in the center velcro tab of the glove.

- One by one, attach the z, e, b, r, a letters onto the glove. Pause between each one, focusing on the sounds

and the blends: z ze zeb zebr zebra. Once "zebra" has been achieved, spell the word by pointing to the letters and saying them out loud.

Name Game

- Have the children think of the name of a person that begins with "z" (Zachary, Zeus, Zizka, etc.).

- Have children work on sentences that focus on the "z" sound (Zachary Zebra is zany at the zoo. Zeus zaps zinc in Zambia. Etc.). Make the sentences as silly as possible.

Finger Plays

- Make five of the zebra finger play characters using the pattern and instructions on page 240.

- Practice rhyming sounds with the finger plays. Use the ones provided, or look for others. Use the finger play characters to count either up or down with the plays.

Count Down Rhyme

"Five Zebras" (Sung to the tune "Twinkle, Twinkle Little Star.")

Five zebras on the African plain,

Black and white from tale to mane.

They roamed at morning, they roamed at night.

One little zebra roamed out of sight.

How many zebras chose to stay?

Let's all count them here today.

Repeat for 4, 3, 2, 1

Count Up Rhyme

"One Little Zebra"

One little zebra, drinking morning dew,

Found another friend, and then there were two.

Two little zebras, prancing wild and free,

Found another friend, and then there were three.

Three little zebras, looking for one more,

Found another friend, and then there were four.

Four little zebras, one more to arrive,

Found another friend, and then there were five.

Resources for Storytime

Use some of these books and poems, or any of your favorites, to create a well-rounded storytime program.

Books

Fontes, Ron. *How the Zebra Got Its Stripes*. Golden Books, 2002. A group of African animals share funny stories about how the zebra got its stripes. Includes facts about why zebras really have stripes.

Gay, Michel. *Zee*. Clarion Books, 2003. Zee tries to wake his sleepy parents; but when the coffee spills, he must find another way to wake them.

Gay, Michel. *Zee is Not Scared*. Houghton Mifflin, 2004. Angry at not being allowed to watch a scary movie with his parents, Zee decides to dress up as a ghost.

McKee, David. *Zebra's Hiccups*. Andersen Press, 2003. When Zebra gets the hiccups, all his animal friends have cures to suggest.

Nunez, Marisa. *Camilla the Zebra*. Illustrated by Oscar Villan. Kalandraka, 2003. When Camilla loses seven of her stripes on a windy day, she receives seven generous replacements.

Paterson, Brian. *Zigby Camps Out*. HarperCollins, 2006. A camping adventure for Zigby and his friends turns into an unforgettable event.

Paterson, Brian. *Zigby Hunts for Treasure.* HarperCollins, 2003. Zigby and his friends go on a treasure hunt to the mysterious Parrot Island.

Peet, Bill. *Zella, Zack and Zodiac.* Houghton Mifflin, 1989. Zella the zebra helps Zack the ostrich when he is young. Zack returns the favor by saving Zella's young offspring from a lion.

Vrombaut, An. *Zed the Zebra.* Hodder & Stoughton, 2008. Zed is faster than any other animal in the jungle—and he's always pointing it out. He is very proud of his go-faster stripes and claims he is the fastest runner in all Africa. But one day the animals plan an obstacle race and prove they can all do something well.

Weninger, Brigitte. *Zara Zebra Draws.* Illustrated by Anna Laura Cantone. North-South Books, 2002. As Zara Zebra draws a variety of shapes, the readers must guess what she is making.

West, Tracey. *Racing Stripes.* Scholastic, 2005. Adapted from the screenplay by David Schmidt.

Poems

"Mrs. Zebra" in *Zig-Zag: Zoems for Zindergarten* by Loris Lesynski. Annick Press, 2004.

"Zebra" in *Wake Up, Sleepy Head!: Early Morning Poems* by Mandy Ross. Illustrated by Dubravka Kolanovic. Child's Play, 2004.

"Zebra Question" in *A Light in the Attic* by Shel Silverstein. HarperCollins, 1981.

"I'm a Little Zebra" (*Sung to the tune "I'm a Little Teapot"*)
I'm a little zebra,
Black and white.
Out on the plains,
In the hot sunlight.
When the day is over,
I'll go home.
Then tomorrow,
Again I'll roam.

Alphabet Activities

ABC Connect-the-Dots

Copy one pattern on page 241 for each child. Have the children connect the dots from A to Z to find the mystery picture.

ABC Striped Zebra

Enlarge and copy one each of the patterns on pages 242–243 for each child. Have the children cut out the individual stripes. The children can match the alphabet stripes to the appropriate spot on the zebra then glue them in place.

Creative Activities

Stand-up Zebra

Copy one zebra pattern from page 244 onto heavy paper for each child. Have the children color in the picture. Cut picture out, and fold on the appropriate line to have a zebra that stands.

Zebra Painting

Cut one zebra shape for each child from white construction paper. Give children cotton swabs and some black paint so they can design their own zebras.

Zebra Roll

Provide each child with a toilet paper roll to make a zebra's body. Using black paint, have the children add stripes. Children can cut and glue heads and legs for their zebras.

Creating Zebra Characters

Make five zebras.

- Trace the zebra pattern onto white fun foam.

- Cut out all the pieces.

- Glue medium-size roly eye to zebra.

- Apply stripes and nose with black fabric paint.

- Braid small pieces of black and white yarn together. Tie.

- Glue the braided yarn to the back of the zebra for a tail.

- Glue small pieces of yarn to the neck for a mane.

- Glue velcro to back.

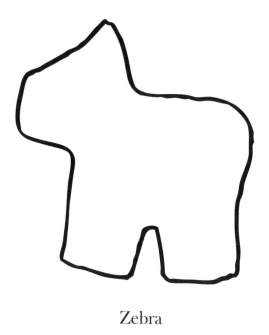

Zebra

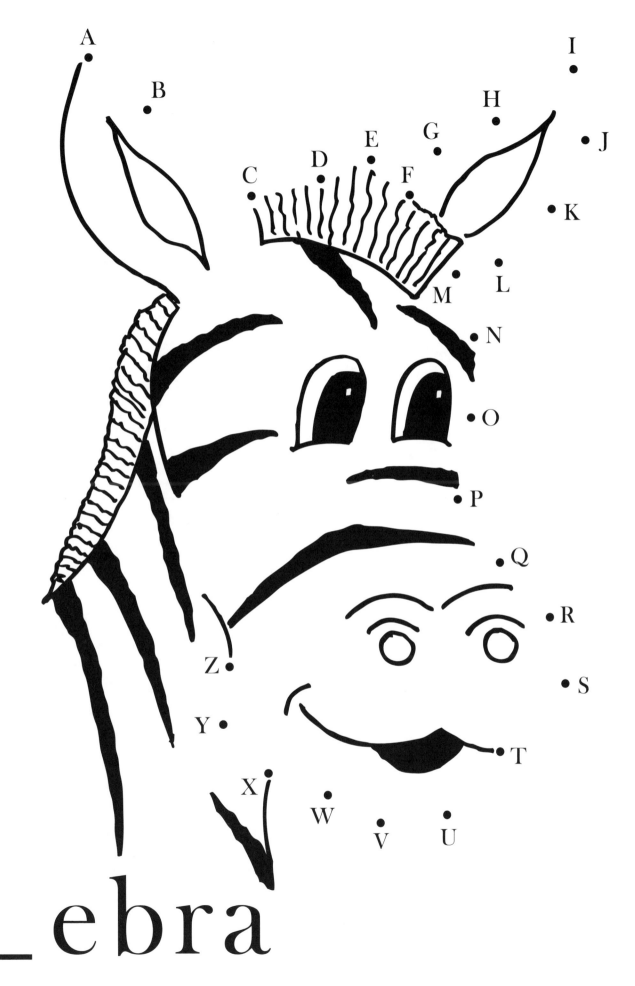

_ebra

Stripe Patterns

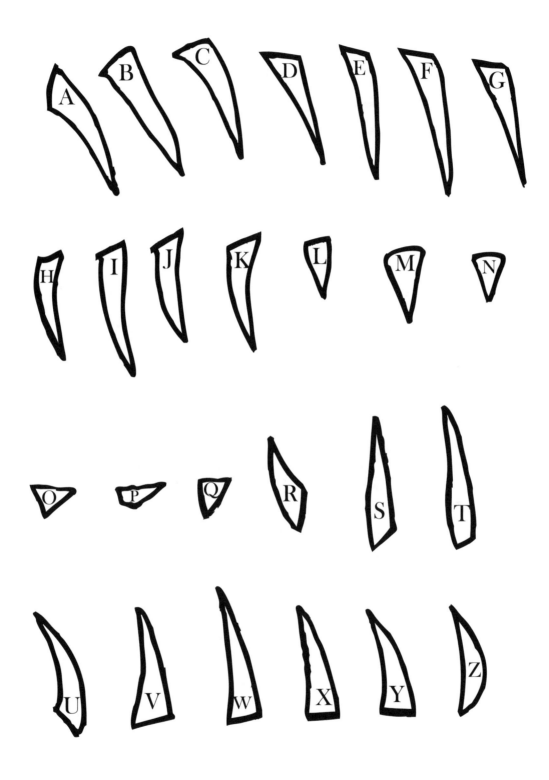

Stand-up Zebra

Z Z Z Z Z Z Z Z Z Z Z

Z Z

Z Z Z Z Z Z Z Z Z Z Z

Z Z

Zz Zz Zz Zz Zz Zz

Zz Zz

ABC Picture Books

You may choose to further strengthen or supplement your programs by introducing alphabet books. The majority of these books introduce each letter of the alphabet with a topical description. These stories can be read for fun at the end of a program, or as a relaxing break at any time.

Bar-el, Can. *Alphabetter.* Illustrated by Graham Ross. Orca, 2006. Children find themselves with the wrong objects, but learn to help each other.

Beccia, Carlyn. *Who Put the B in the Ballyhoo?* Houghton Mifflin, 2007. A rhyming alphabetical description of Big Top life and attractions, interspersed with facts about particular circus acts and personalities of the past.

Bonder, Dianna. *Dogabet.* Walrus Books, 2007. Features aristocratic Afghans, donut dunking Dachshunds and yodeling Yorkies.

Edwards, Wallace. *Alphabeasts.* Kids Can Press, 2002. A unique, imaginative, artistic look at the alphabet.

Ernst, Lisa Campbell. *The Turn-Around Upside-Down Alphabet Book.* Simon & Schuster, 2004. An alphabet book in which each letter becomes three different objects as the book is turned different directions, as when A becomes a bird's beak, a drippy ice cream cone, and the point of a star.

Gaiman, Neil. *The Dangerous Alphabet.* HarperCollins, 2008. A tale of adventure, piracy, danger, and heroism told in twenty-six alphabetical lines—although even the alphabet is not to be relied upon here. Sure to captivate and chill young readers.

Goldsberry, U'ilani. *A is for Aloha: A Hawai'i Alphabet.* Sleeping Bear Press, 2005. One of a series of alphabet books on the States.

Haas, Jessie. *Appaloosa Zebra: A Horse Lover's Alphabet.* Illustrated by Margot Apple. Greenwillow Books, 2002. Moving through the alphabet, a girl ponders the many different kinds of horses she will have when she gets older, from Appaloosa to Zebra.

Isadora, Rachel. *On Your Toes: A Ballet ABC.* Greenwillow Books, 2003. Each letter of the alphabet is represented by an illustration of a ballet-related word.

Jocelyn, Marthe. *ABC x 3: English, Español, Français.* Illustrated by Tom Slaughter. Tundra Books, 2005. Deceptively simple paper cuts will delight the eye while young readers explore words in three languages.

Kontis, Alethea. *Alpha Oops: The Day Z went First.* Illustrated by Bob Kolar. Candlewick Press, 2006. Z is tired of always being last, but his latest rebellion sparks some surprising consequences.

Lear, Edward. *A Was Once an Apple Pie.* Illustrated by Suse MacDonald. Orchard Books, 2005. Lively illustrations bring Lear's well-known poem to life.

Lewis, Jan. *Dinosaur 123 ABC!* Scholastic, 2004. A is for apple and Apatosaurus to Z is for zigzag and Zephyrosaurus.

Lohnes, Marilyn. *F is for Fiddlehead: A New Brunswick Alphabet.* Illustrated by Susan Tooke. Sleeping Bear Press, 2007. One of the series in progress of alphabet books on the Canadian provinces.

Martin, Bill Jr. *Chicka Chicka Boom Boom.* Aladdin, 2000. An alphabet rhyme/chant that relates what happens when the whole alphabet tries to climb a coconut tree.

McLeod, Bob. *Superhero ABC.* HarperCollins, 2006. Humorous SuperHeroes such as Goo Girl and The Volcano represent the letters of the alphabet from A to Z.

McLimans, David. *Gone Wild: An Endangered Animal Alphabet.* Walker & Co., 2006. Endangered animals are cleverly incorporated into alphabet letters.

Nickle, John. *Alphabet Explosion.* Schwartz & Wade Books, 2006. Readers search and count the number of objects beginning with each letter.

Pallotta, Jerry. *The Jet Alphabet Book.* Illustrated by Rob Bolster. Charlesbridge, 2002. An alphabet book presenting unusual facts about a variety of jet planes, from the Airocomet to the Zephyr.

Paul, Ann. *Eight Hands Round: A Patchwork Alphabet.* Illustrated by Jeanette Winter. HarperCollins, 1996. Introduces the letters of the alphabet with names of early American patchwork quilt patterns and explains the origins of the designs by describing the activity or occupation they derive from.

Prieto, Anita C. *B is for Bookworm: A Library Alphabet.* Illustrated by Renée

Graef. Sleeping Bear Press, 2005. One of a series of alphabet books about careers. See also *T is for Teachers.*

Slater, Teddy. *ABC Sing-Along.* Illustrated by Liisa Chauncy Guida. Scholastic, 2006. Songs with familiar tunes and pull tabs introduce letters of the alphabet. Includes CD.

Sobel, June. *B is for Bulldozer: A Construction ABC.* Illustrated by Melissa Iwai. Voyager Books, 2003. As children watch over the course of a year, builders construct a rollercoaster using tools and materials that begin with each letter of the alphabet.

Ulmer, Mike. *J is for Jump Shot: A Basketball Alphabet.* Illustrated by Mark Braught. Sleeping Bear Press, 2005. One of a series of sports alphabet books by Sleeping Bear Press.

Van Fleet, Matthew. *Alphabet.* Simon & Schuster, 2008. Over 100 creatures and plants from A to Z hilariously demonstrate action words, synonyms, opposites, and more. An interactive book.

Wells, Rosemary. *Max's ABC.* Penguin Young Readers, 2006. The loveable bunny siblings return with an introduction to alphabet concepts.

Resources

Any storytime program starts with planning and preparation. In addition to this book, you may wish to look at other resources and styles of programming, including flannelboards, puppetry, introductory phonics, and educational activities. This list also includes sources consulted while creating this book.

Bouchard, David. *For the Love of Reading: Books to Build Lifelong Readers*. Orca Books, 2004. Literacy experts create lists of inspiring books for children.

Briggs, Diane. *52 Programs for Preschoolers: The Librarian's Year-Round Planner*. ALA Editions, 1997. A number of useful themes to follow.

Briggs, Diane. *101 Fingerplays, Stories, and Songs to use with Finger Puppets*. ALA Editions, 1999. Finger puppets are presented in a variety of ways.

Chalufour, Ingrid, and Karen Worth. *Discovering Nature with Young Children*. Redleaf Press, 2003. An early introduction to science and science principles.

Charlesworth, Lisa. *A Xylophone for X-Ray Fish*. Scholastic, 2000. A series of 26 animal storybooks that build phonemic awareness.

Church, Ellen Booth, with Deb Hensley. *The Great Big Book of Classroom Songs, Rhymes, and Cheers: 200 Easy, Playful Language Experiences that Build Literacy and Community in Your Classroom*. Scholastic Professional, 2000. Ideas for various levels of learners.

The Complete Book of the Alphabet. McGraw Hill Children's Publishing, 2004. Lessons and activities to teach and reinforce the alphabet to preschool children.

Crepeau, Ingrid M., and M. Ann Richards. *A Show of Hands: Using Puppets with Young Children*. Redleaf Press, 2003. Innovative ways to use puppets as teaching tools.

Everything for Early Learning. School Specialty Publishing, 2004. Fun games, activities, and puzzles to help build a foundation of reading, language arts, and mathematical skills for preschoolers. See also the kindergarten workbook.

Ghoting, Saroj Nadkarni, and Pamela Martin-Diaz. *Early Literacy Storytimes @ Your Library: Partnering with Caregivers for Success.* ALA Editions, 2005. Though not one of the books I used as a reference to this book, it sounds quite interesting. By presenting storytimes designed for both children and adults, librarians model how to choose books, share them, and encourage the skills that children need when they start school.

Gilbert, LaBritta. *50 Great Make-it, Take-it Projects.* UpstartBooks, 2001. Easy-to-make projects for K–5.

Hodges, Di. *365 TV-Free Activities for Toddlers.* Hinkler Books Pty. Ltd., 2003. Includes sections on enhancing language skills.

Lohnes, Marilyn. *Finger Folk.* Alleyside Press, 1999. Fingerplay characters and rhymes for storytime themes.

Marsh, Valerie. *Stories that Stick: Quick and Easy Storyboard Tales.* UpstartBooks, 2001. Storytime scripts and patterns to use with flannelboards or other surfaces.

Miskin, Ruth. *Superphonics.* Hodder Children's Books, 2000. Introduces the alphabet and the sound each letter makes.

My First Book of Lowercase Letters. Kumon Pub. Co. Ltd., 2004. Designed for children ages 4–6 who are starting to learn the alphabet. One of a series of Kumon books including reading, writing, and math skills.

Novelli, Joan. *Irresistible A,B,Cs.* Scholastic Professional Books, 2000. Fifty activities designed to help children explore the alphabet and learn the letters.

Press, Judy. *ArtStarts for Little Hands!* Illustrated by Karol Kaminski. Williamson Publishing, 2000. A variety of themed projects and activities.

Rousseau, Lina and Robert Chiasson. *Lire à des enfants et animer la lecture.* Les éditions ASTED, 2004. Techniques to promote simple and fun ways of making reading fun.

Schiller, Pam, and Jackie Sillberg. *The Complete Book of Activities, Games, Stories, Props, Recipes, and Dances for Young Children.* Gryphon House, 2002. Over 600 selections in this title.

Sher, Barbara. *Smart Play: 101 Fun, Easy Games that Enhance Intelligence.* Illustrated by Ralph Butler. John Wiley & Sons, 2004. Educational games used in family recreation help to stimulate intellectual abilities.

Sipe, Lawrence R. *Storytime: Young Children's Literacy Understanding in the Classroom.* Teacher's College Press, 2007. Built on a solid theoretical and research foundation, *Storytime* gives the reader deep insight into how young children construct literary understanding in the context of picture storybooks.

Spann, Mary Beth. *Learn-the-Alphabet Puppet Pals.* Scholastic Professional Books, 2003. Stick puppets introduce letters of the alphabet.

Totten, Kathryn. *Fantastic, Fun Reading Programs.* UpstartBooks, 2001. Forty fun, original programs.

Totten, Kathryn. *Seasonal Storytime Crafts.* UpstartBooks, 2002. Crafts that highlight holidays, special days, and weather.

Wepner, Shelley, et. al, eds. *Linking Literacy and Technology: A Guide for K–8 Classrooms.* International Reading Association, 2000. Focuses on the uses of computer technology in promoting literacy skills.

Willenken, Roberta. *Learn-the-Alphabet Arts & Crafts.* Scholastic Professional Books, 2000. Activities designed to create take-home ABC books.

Yopp, Hallie Kay, and Ruth Helen Yopp. "Supporting Phonemic Awareness Development in the Classroom." *The Reading Teacher,* vol. 54, no. 2 (October, 2000). pp. 130–143.